GO STRAIGHT ON
PEACHTREE

Anne Rivers Siddons

GO STRAIGHT ON
PEACHTREE

A McDonald City Guide

DOLPHIN BOOKS
DOUBLEDAY & COMPANY, INC.
GARDEN CITY, NEW YORK
1978

Library of Congress Cataloging in Publication Data

Siddons, Anne Rivers.
  Go straight on Peachtree.

  Includes index.
    1. Atlanta—Description—Guide-books.
  2. Atlanta region, Ga.—Description and travel—
  Guide-books.   I. Title.
  F294.A83S53   917.58′231′044
  ISBN 0-385-11144-4
  Library of Congress Catalog Card Number 76-16257

Contents

List of Maps

GO STRAIGHT ON
PEACHTREE

This Place Called Atlanta

Perhaps, after all is said and done, it took Margaret Mitchell to sum us up best. In her beloved *Gone with the Wind,* she has an exasperated Mammy accuse a balky Scarlett O'Hara of being "a mule dressed up in hoss harness."

She put her finger on the city for good and all.

Atlanta is an upstart. A lusty country lass come late to town, with lace on her parasol and red clay on her petticoats. Wise, now, in the ways of the world; a rich girl, a sophisticated lady wheeling and dealing and playing with the world's great and near great, who come courting in endless streams. But a hoyden, for all that. Vital and brash and charismatic and full of joy and vinegar. Very beautiful, very modern. And very young.

This rolling green earth where Atlanta lives is old earth; our Indian heritage goes back into the mists of prehistory. And at the time that our graceful, languorous sister cities of the South—dreaming Savannah, blue-blooded Charleston—were old, the land by the Chattahoochee River that would become Atlanta was still the province of wild things, virgin forests, and the Creek and Cherokee nations, whose territories the great, brown river divided. Our first official citizen didn't make his appearance until 1833; his name was Hardy Ivy, and he hacked himself a homestead out of the wilderness near a red clay crossroad on a likely hilltop. Today, we call it Five Points. It's the essential heart of the city.

There were white men in these hills long before Hardy Ivy took an ax to the timber at Five Points. During the War of 1812, the Creek Nation formed an alliance with the British. In order to keep them at bay, American troops constructed two forts, Fort Daniels and Fort Peachtree, near the Indian trading post called "Standing Peachtree," at the mouth of Peachtree Creek, at the Chattahoochee River. The thirty-mile road connecting the two fortifications became the original Peachtree Road, and it cost its contractors $150.

But it was really the railroads that built us, and the railroads that tore us down; Atlanta and the railroads have always had a strange love affair going. As the rails crept in from north, east, south, and west, the settlement evolved into a flourishing transportation center and became known, logically enough, as Terminus. In 1843, it was renamed Marthasville, after the daughter of Governor Wilson Lumpkin, and in 1845, an engineer of the Georgia railroad suggested "Atlanta" as a female form of "Atlantic," since the town was the western terminus of the Western and Atlantic Railroad. The legislature confirmed the new name in 1847, much to the chagrin of Governor Lumpkin, who declared the change to be the result of "low envy" on the part of others. Nobody seems to know what daughter Martha thought about the whole thing.

At any rate, Atlanta was, by the time the Civil War geared up, a thriving small city of more than twenty thousand people, and what was more important—and ominous —a rail and manufacturing center supplying the armies of the Confederacy. Her death warrant was signed long before the first shot was fired at Fort Sumter, at Charleston Harbor.

The siege of Atlanta is known throughout the world, thanks to Miss Mitchell's monumental and magnificent book. . . . Atlanta was left in ruins. Few buildings stood. Her rails were twisted into knots called "Sherman's neckties," her depots and warehouses leveled, her residences and businesses in ashes and rubble, her citizens evacuated. It's said that when Sherman's troops rode out of town on the Jonesboro road, on a pale November morning in 1864, to start the legendary March to the Sea, the troops broke into a crashing chorus of "The Battle Hymn of the Republic." It's also said that the first contingent going out met the first wave of Atlantans coming back—on foot and in mule carts—to rebuild their city and their lives.

And rebuild it they did, in an incredibly short time, through a bitter Reconstruction, two world wars, a crippling Depression, the periods of flaming social change and upheaval that marked our mid-century period. Rebuilt it into the proud, supercharged, international city of almost two million people we are today.

The Atlanta you will meet is a unique, humming, throbbing city of trade, transportation, warehousing, branch offices, headquarters, finance and real estate, legendary shopping and wining and dining and cultural activities, and more attractions, activities, and inklings and oddments than you could taste in a year. It's full of turbans, djellabas, Hare Krishna robes, and Arab money. We hope you will savor today's aspect of the city—cosmopolitan, crackling, elegant, rowdy, on fire with change. But we also hope you will not forget yesterday's; it's all around you, in Atlanta.

Physically, Atlanta is a very beautiful city; we are fond of saying that we have the world's loveliest residential sections, and we've had few challengers. On a spring day when the white lace of our famous dogwood drifts on the city's shoulders like snow, it does not seem an unreasonable claim. Our bronze autumns are mild and beautiful too, and our winters are splendid with the bare traceries of the sea of trees that laps into our very center. And our summers are deep and green and seldom searing. I revel in the beauty of my city, but I like its grit and sweat and smells and noise, too. This living, breathing city is very real to me.

Marge McDonald, my friend and associate whose idea this book was to begin with and whose expertise you will meet on every page, is a relative newcomer, from the East, and a multi-talented and energetic woman who founded one of the best and most respected tour-and-convention service organizations in the South. Marge is now president of the Georgia Hospitality and Travel Ass'n. She sees this city in a different light from mine. From her unique vantage point as an Easterner and an innovative total professional, she knows Atlanta inside out. You will be seeing this city, for the great part, through her eyes.

From my vantage point as a native and writer—an introspective creature at best—I hope you will see it, in part, the way I do: from the inside of *me* out. Atlanta is a place of textures and impressions, tastes and sights and sounds, memories and bone-deep, back-of-the-neck awareness. To me, Atlanta is the peculiar purple of a winter sky over the woods behind my house, like the sheen of a grape. It is languid summers woven of Coca-Cola and iced tea and gently shabby old clubs. It is the bronze, MGM falls made of football and hot dogs at Grant Stadium, the stars in the ceiling at the Fox Theatre, the resigned grin of a total stranger stuck in traffic next to me on the early-morning Expressway, the Christmas lights in Saks and Lord & Taylor's and Neiman-Marcus. It is memories that go back a long, long way: being frightened out of my wits passing a Ku Klux Klan rally on a vast, windy, black night at Stone Mountain; driving my red sports car giddily down the green spring canyons of the Northwest, tires squealing, singing at the top of my lungs; watching the sorrowful train that bore the body of the first President I ever knew back from Warm Springs to Washington, at the old Union Station downtown; the half-comprehended horror of the great Winecoff Hotel fire.

Atlanta has, for me, a sense of place like nowhere else on earth. It is my place, my city, my earth. It will be yours, now, for a day, a week, or longer.

As my Irish forebears used to say, I wish you joy of it.

About This Book

We've called this book *Go Straight on Peachtree* because that's precisely what we intend it to help you do: decide what you want to see and do, and get there as easily and comfortably as possible. We've heard it over and over, from visitors and newcomers: "How can we best see Atlanta without joining a formal tour? Why doesn't somebody help the individual or family who has a car and some free time and knows nothing whatsoever about the city?" We hope this guide will do just that.

Atlanta is a big city, an enormous one. If you drive around downtown, you're going to spend most of your time trying to get yourself unlost, and see only a little of it. If you make a foray into some of the residential sections, you could easily miss the most beautiful, the most interesting, the most historic, the most significant ones—and run out of gas, to boot. If you want to go shopping, who's going to tell you where the best shops are? If you want to dine out or paint the town, where are you going to find the best of what you're looking for?

Here, we hope.

In this guide, we've divided the city into sections. Not only geographical sections, but areas of interest for just about everybody. We've put together several tours in each category, tours that are logical, practical, and easy to drive, and we've given you explicit driving directions for each one, along with approximate times for each. There are short tours and daylong ones; we've even suggested places to lunch or dine along the way in most, and given a brief description and history of each attraction on each tour. These directions have been double-checked for accuracy.

All you need in order to see the best of Atlanta are this book and a car.

As you'll see from the table of Contents, we have general tours that will get you acquainted with the major historical, civic, recreational, and cultural attractions of Atlanta. Tours of particular interest to children and families. Special tours for all kinds of shopping, antiquing, and boutiquing. Tours to acquaint you with the city's galleries and museums, our restored areas. There are walking tours too, and all manner of unusual and noteworthy sites that, perhaps, don't fall into a logical tour but shouldn't be missed. You'll find these in the *et cetera* sections following the chapters where they apply.

For nighttime doings, we've told you all about our cultural attractions, theatre, dance, opera, dinner theatres, concert halls . . . and suggested some places to park, places for dinner, places for late suppers and nightcaps. And we've put together several evening tours that will take you from ante-bellum days to big and elegant bistros, and everything in between.

We have a comprehensive section on sports you see and one on sports you do, a complete listing of annual special events that light up the city, and several tours that take you to the best of our out-of-town attractions and bring you back again.

Then there are suggested restaurants and night spots, a complete list of hotel and motel facilities in and around the city, and a helpful section on weather and clothes.

Near the back, you'll find a page of admissions and hours for major attractions. There's also a page of general directions for the places you'll encounter most frequently. And, of course, each tour in this book has its own directions, set into the narrative, so you can follow them as you come to them. Wherever a phone number is necessary, it is listed, and there are pages of maps, so you can begin to orient yourself before you set out.

This is not a complete and total index of Atlanta. It was not intended to be an encyclopedic work. Rather, we hope it will help you find what you're most interested in, and get you there and back with a minimum of fuss and bother. We've covered every conceivable area of the city, from its history to its hostelries, but selectively. Rather than deluge you with information, we hope we've stimulated you to get out, explore, sample, savor, and experience this city we love to its fullest. We've made it easy to do. Pick your subject or do it all. *Go Straight on Peachtree* is designed to help you do both, on your own.

Daytime Atlanta

You could use up a lifetime—or several—trying to exhaust the resources of Atlanta under the sun. It sparkles, crackles, hums, roars; it soothes you and sings to you, amuses you, touches you, exhilarates you, enchants you, and not infrequently infuriates you. It never bores you. There is the electricity of Atlanta's dynamic downtown, the mannered grace of her velvety residential sections, the cloistered peace and twentieth-century verve of her great academic centers, the charm of small, beguiling boutiques, the stately spell of dim, rich antique shops and galleries, the cheeky elegance of her great fashion houses.

Atlanta's rich, brawling, and ultimately lovely past lingers on, alive and well in museums and restorations, battlefields and history-haunted villages and settlements, columned old houses and bowery gardens. Past and present mingle happily in heart-lifting attractions such as Underground Atlanta, Six Flags over Georgia, and Stone Mountain. And our future blazes vividly from the towers of such futuristic complexes as Peachtree Center, Colony Square, and Omni International. No city in America, perhaps, spans so many eras of history so gracefully . . . or offers its history so openhandedly to visitor and native alike.

In the Daytime Atlanta section of this book, we'll try to spread you a tempting *smörgåsbord* of things to do, see, and experience by day in and around the city, including general tours designed to acquaint you with all our faces, special enchantments for kids, a fine gaggle of shopping, art, and museum forays, restorations, driving and walking tours, and a glittering welter of inklings and oddments that don't quite fit any categories but are just too good to miss. Pick your own interest or sample them all. Atlanta, first and foremost, is more fun than just about anywhere under the sun.

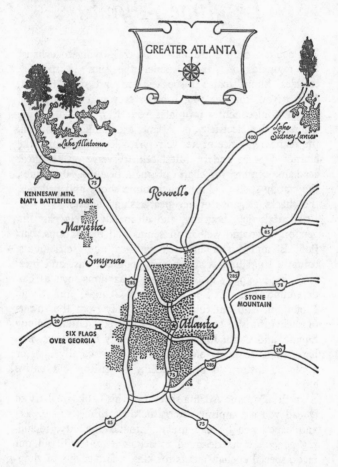

GENERAL TOURS

Whether you want to savor the entire city in one grand, fell swoop, spend a day in our fascinating, eclectic downtown, get acquainted with the elegance that was—and still is—ours, please your entire family for an entire day, combine the crackle of the city with the peace of the country, wander through the enchanting world that lies at the base of the world's largest granite mountain, retrace General Sherman's march through Atlanta and walk the legend-haunted battlefields of the Civil War in *Gone with the Wind* country, or explore Atlanta's rich, many-faceted black heritage . . . you'll find it here.

THE ONCE AND FUTURE ATLANTA
(*7 to 9 hours*)
A loving, leisurely look at Atlanta over-all: how we've lived and worked and played, from our graceful ante-bellum days to now . . . and a glimpse into our shining tomorrows. Take all or part of the tour; it's the best way to see us as we were, are, and will be, and you won't forget any of it.

A point of interest along the way: The Fox Theatre, at Third Street and Peachtree, which is opened for special events and tours. It's one of the country's great movie palaces, with fantastic Moorish architecture, opulent 1920s interiors, and stars that twinkle from the ceiling.

From downtown, go north on Peachtree (right fork at Baker Street) to 15th Street, and park in the garage under the Atlanta Memorial Arts Center, just past 15th Street.

Once you're parked, cross the street and stroll through Colony Square, a futuristic complex of offices, shops, and condominiums and the Colony Square Hotel. Browse through the shops and boutiques, wander through the Colony Square Hotel, with its many restaurants and lounges.

Then visit the Atlanta Memorial Arts Center, across the

street. Walk through the soaring Galleria, reflect for a moment on Rodin's magnificent *L'Ombre* (The Shade), sent to us by France as a memorial to the 122 Atlantans who died in an air crash in Paris in 1962. It's on the steps, by the museum entrance. Then savor the rest of the excellent museum. If you have youngsters along, a charming exhibit on the third floor is just for them. Now on to the beautiful Northwest section of Atlanta and the Atlanta Historical Society.

Leave the Arts Center garage, L Lombardy, R 15th Street, R West Peachtree, L Peachtree for about 2 miles, L Peachtree Battle, R Habersham, R Cherokee, L Andrews, R through the gates of the Historical Society.

Atlanta's legendary Northside has often been called the most beautiful residential section in the country. As you drive, you'll see elegant dowager houses set far back on velvet lawns under vaulting old trees. As you turn into the Historical Society grounds, you'll see the best of Atlanta's rich, shimmering past, lovingly restored to its former luster. Visit the meticulously restored Tullie Smith House, a Georgia farmer's home, circa 1840. Tour the palatial, rococo Swan House, a Palladian villa built in 1928 by noted Atlanta architect Philip Shutze, crowning the highest green hill on the Historical Society's eighteen deeply wooded acres. The spectacular new headquarters of the Historical Society brims with art, artifacts, and exhibits. Browse in the Coach House, the restored servants' quarters of the Swan House, now an excellent art gallery and gift shop. Lunch in the Coach House restaurant is delightful; it's a fine place to join "old Atlanta," and it's moderately priced. Or you might want to lunch at Brennan's, the famed New Orleans restaurant.

Go out the back gate of the Historical Society, turn R on West Paces Ferry for Brennan's.

After lunch, continue exploring Atlanta's enchanting Northside. Head west on West Paces Ferry Road. On your right, atop a green knoll, is the Georgia Governor's Mansion, surrounded by formal gardens and accented by a splashing fountain. The mansion's interior is furnished with authentic pieces from Georgia's past.

R Tuxedo, R at fork, L Blackland.

This part of the tour will take you past some of the most spectacular of Atlanta's many famous stately homes. The white-columned house set far back on the sweeping lawn behind the iron gates to your right on Blackland is said to be the most photographed residence in Atlanta. Now let's go downtown.

Turn L on Northside Drive, R West Paces Ferry, L I-75 South (under the bridge), through downtown Atlanta, exit Dr. Martin Luther King Blvd.

The shiny gold dome on your left is the State Capitol building, and that's real gold, brought from the hills of Dahlonega, in North Georgia. Surrounding the Capitol are state office buildings. Two blocks after you exit on Martin Luther King Boulevard, you're at the entrance to Underground Atlanta, our unique "city beneath the city." It's an authentic restoration of the actual shops, saloons, and cafés that served Atlanta in the colorful, brawling 1850s, when she was a rail center without peer. Streets and rail viaducts gradually grew up over this section, driving it underground into obscurity, but it's been reawakened into one of the great attractions in the South. Here are the gaslights and cobblestones, the nickelodeons and nickel lunches, the saloons and sundry shops that sustained and amused our forebears. Wander at will in the fascinating maze of shops and boutiques and museums, have a snack at one of a score of charming cafés and restaurants. It's all real. Now for the Omni.

From Underground Atlanta parking, go straight on MLK Blvd., R on Techwood, parking on right.

The incredible world of the Omni International dominates Atlanta's western downtown area. This megastructure contains a luxury hotel, several of the city's finest restaurants and lounges, movie theatres, international luxury shopping and a European-type shopping bazaar, and an enormous ice-skating rink. It's all under one "skin," and adjacent to it, connected by covered walkways, is the Omni sports arena, where the Atlanta Flames and the Atlanta Hawks dispense major-league ice hockey and basketball, and the world's brightest entertainers hold forth regularly. If you've time, do explore it all. But save time and room for Peachtree Center, coming up next.

From the Omni, continue on Techwood, L Marietta, R International Blvd., L Spring, R Harris Park.

Peachtree Center, our vibrant, new-as-tomorrow city within a city, is one of the premier stars in our downtown crown. Architect John Portman created this soaring world, with its co-ordinated structures, parks, plazas, outdoor cafés, restaurants and lounges, theatres and nightclubs, offices and shops. And the whole world is copying it—a pretty good sign that the Atlanta of today may be the international city of tomorrow. Park and stroll around, both at ground level and through the maze of building-to-building crosswalks in midair. Finally, cross the bridge from the shopping mall of Peachtree Center to the Hyatt Regency Atlanta, and take the soaring glass bubble elevator in the lobby to the revolving glass Polaris Lounge, twenty-three stories above the city. A quiet drink here is an unforgettable experience.

Or take the outside elevator at the Peachtree Plaza Hotel, across the street (it's the world's tallest hotel), and soar seventy heart-lifting stories to the revolving lounge at the top. Here, with a cool drink before you and all of Atlanta at your feet, you might reflect that today you've seen the Atlanta of yesterday, today, and tomorrow . . . and from here you can see them all. Welcome.

DYNAMIC DOWNTOWN
(*2 hours, 5 hours, all day, or several days, as you like it*)
Atlanta is a city with one foot in fact and one in legend . . . and often the fact is fully as fascinating as the lovely, graceful legends. For all its lingering spell of crinolines, columns, and dreaming green lawns, Atlanta is very much

a city of today and tomorrow, crackling with verve and muscle and excitement . . . and most of it is generated downtown. Drive it, walk it, sample it; downtown Atlanta is like no other place on earth. A note: wear walking shoes!

Start at Peachtree Center, the complex that changed Atlanta's skyline (and the world's mind about Atlanta). It's in the middle of downtown Atlanta, at Peachtree Street and International Boulevard.

If you're staying in the northern area of Atlanta, take I-75/I-85 South, exit Courtland, R International 3 blocks to parking. From southern Atlanta, I-75/I-85 North, exit International, 2 to 3 blocks to parking. If you're staying east or west of the city, go to I-20, exit I-85 North, exit International and Peachtree.

Park your car and walk through the interconnecting plazas studded with sculpture. The new Peachtree Plaza Hotel crowns the Center from seventy stories up. At the other end of Peachtree Center is the hotel that first began generating the Center's electricity: the famed Hyatt Regency Atlanta, with its soaring, lushly planted interior lobby, its lounges and restaurants, and its unique revolving Polaris Lounge atop it all. The whole of Peachtree Center is a treasure trove of boutiques, restaurants and cafés featuring international cuisine, planted flowering walks and vistas. See it all, then back to the car.

From Peachtree Street, go 2 blocks E to Courtland, turn R, turn L on Auburn, continue on Auburn 4 blocks.

If you're on Harris Street before you turn onto Courtland, or if you exited Courtland from I-75/I-85, you'll see the Atlanta Center Limited, another of our fast-rising total urban complexes. Here are offices, shops and boutiques, restaurants, and the new Hilton Hotel, Atlanta's largest, boasting four tennis courts and a jogging track and health club. Stop and browse a bit if you like. You'll soon see that Atlanta is a city with many centers in its heart.

On Auburn, you're on a street of totally black-owned

businesses, one of the nation's first. Auburn Avenue has been a thriving commercial thoroughfare since the turn of the century. Also on this street is the headquarters of the Southern Christian Leadership Conference, founded by Atlanta Nobel Peace Prize winner Dr. Martin Luther King, Jr. Four blocks from Courtland Street on Auburn is the Ebenezer Baptist Church, where Dr. King shared the pulpit with his father, Atlanta's beloved "Daddy King." And adjacent to the church is the gravesite of Dr. King, Jr., where an eternal flame now burns to the memory of this remarkable man. One block farther on Auburn is the birthplace of Martin Luther King, Jr., now open to the public.

After visiting Dr. King's birthplace, L Hogue, L Irwin, R Boulevard, L I-485 in the middle of the bridge, follow I-85 South, exit MLK Blvd.

As you come to I-485, and if traffic permits, pause a moment on the bridge. You'll have one of the city's best views of Atlanta's skyline. Then, as you exit MLK Boulevard, you'll see the gold dome of the Georgia State Capitol, gilded with real Georgia gold brought from the hills of North Georgia, where one of the country's first gold rushes took place. The Capitol grounds are always a sea of color, with plants and flowers rioting in each season. The Capitol has daily tours, if you're interested. Ask in the lobby. Many of the state office buildings surrounding the Capitol are built of marble quarried in Georgia. On your left as you exit is the Georgia Archives Building—the great white windowless monolith. Georgia's history lies here, in art, artifacts, and records. The daily tours are truly fascinating.

From MLK Blvd., L Washington, L Trinity, L Memorial (and R Capitol Ave. if you wish to visit the Archives), L MLK Blvd., cross Washington and park on the right. You have just circled the Capitol.

As you take this circle, on your right, on Mitchell Street across Washington, is the Atlanta City Hall. As you walk to the right on MLK Boulevard, after parking, you'll see the entrance to Underground Atlanta. Before you visit Underground Atlanta, notice on your left the old Immaculate Conception Church. The original Catholic church stood here during General Sherman's march into Atlanta, and its first pastor, Father O'Reilly, is credited with convincing the general to spare the city's churches. A plaque in memory of Father O'Reilly is situated on the grounds of the Atlanta City Hall. In the block from Central Avenue to Pryor are the Fulton County Courthouse and office buildings. This entire area of Atlanta is known as the Tri-Governmental complex and is one of the only such city-county-state government office complexes in the United States.

Now for Underground Atlanta, on the right from where you parked. This fascinating "city beneath the city" is far better seen than described. It's an authentic restoration of an entire area of the city that brawled and bloomed when the railroads were in flower, complete with the shops, saloons, and cafés that flourished then. Atlanta had its beginning in this old area when railroaders drove a post into the ground to mark the terminus of the Western & Atlantic Railroad and called it Zero Milepost. You can still see Zero Milepost today in Underground Atlanta, along with cobbled streets lined with boutiques, cafés, saloons, museums, exhibits, and restaurants of all sizes and descriptions. It makes a good lunch stop. And at night, gaslight and music and laughter bring it all alive.

After you visit Underground Atlanta, continue on MLK Blvd., R on Techwood, R on Marietta, L on Peachtree at the First National Bank Building, continue straight (Peachtree runs into Edgewood), L on Ivy.

As you're driving up Martin Luther King Boulevard, you'll pass a truly great old Atlanta landmark, Rich's beloved department store, at the corner of Broad Street and Martin Luther King. Rich's is a fashion pace setter, a household word, an Atlanta institution . . . it's always first in the hearts of Atlantans.

Then, as you turn on Techwood, the incredible Omni

International complex is on your left. Omni International Atlanta houses a futuristic sports arena (home of the Atlanta Flames hockey team and Atlanta Hawks basketball team), a 500-room luxury hotel, a huge ice-skating rink, many levels of boutiques and luxury shopping, movie theatres, many fine international restaurants. All in all, the Omni is simply not to be missed.

After you turn right on Marietta, you'll soon come to Atlanta's financial district, humming heart of this new international city. And also on Marietta Street, at Forsyth Street, you'll see the statue of Henry Grady, one of our great statesmen and newspaper editors, who, after the Civil War, coined the phrase "Atlanta, a city too busy to hate."

Continue on Ivy, L International, R Peachtree, straight ahead at fork onto West Peachtree (about 2 blocks), R at 5th St., L Peachtree.

At West Peachtree and Fifth streets, you'll see still another Atlanta landmark, the lovely old Sheraton Biltmore Hotel. In the gentler twenties and thirties, debutantes bowed and Atlanta society played in the grand salon and ballrooms, and scores of theatrical and operatic personalities were entertained in the formal gardens hung with Japanese lanterns. Now, in the elegant Empire Suite, the Wits End Players present their bitingly funny revues nightly and for matinees.

When you turn left on Peachtree Street, you'll be in a colorful area long known as "Tight Squeeze." It was so named because, in Atlanta's frontier days, bandits lurked here in the forests, and citizens riding north were lucky to get through with their money and belongings, not to mention their lives. During the sixties, it was the home of Atlanta's colorful community of hippies and flower children, and it now houses numerous small shops and businesses.

Further out Peachtree, on your right at Fourteenth Street, is the intriguing world of Colony Square, billed as the city's first micropolis. Colony Square, a beautifully designed complex of town houses, offices, boutiques, and restaurants, houses the enormously popular Colony Square Hotel. It's all centered around a giant ice rink . . . take a spin, if your ankles are up to it. By all means, roam through the Colony Square Hotel and perhaps have a snack or a cool drink in one of the many restaurants or lounges.

On your left, at Peachtree and Fifteenth streets, stands the shining white Atlanta Memorial Arts Center, which houses the fine High Museum of Art, the Atlanta Symphony, the Alliance Theatre and smaller Studio Theatre, and the Atlanta School of Art. This unique structure was completed in 1968, in memory of 122 Atlanta art patrons who were killed in an air crash in Paris, and is a true cultural center for the Southeast. It's a lovely hour's browse.

This, then, is downtown Atlanta: muscle and bustle, grace and languor, history and heritage and vision.

To return downtown, take a short detour through lovely, tree-shaded old Ansley Park, one of the city's oldest and most exquisitely restored in-town residential neighborhoods. R 15th St., L Peachtree Circle, R Westminster, R The Prado, R Piedmont 2 miles to the center of downtown.

ALL OVER TOWN
(1½ to 2 hours)
If you've only a little time but you'd like to see a lot of city, this tour is for you. It will keep you in your car only a couple of hours at most, but, of course, you can stop off anywhere that takes your fancy if you have a few minutes to spare. Let's go: from our crackling downtown to our booming midsections to our graceful Northwest, and back again. One thought: since you will be driving, you'll want to bring along a navigator/commentator. This sweep of the city is too good to miss a moment . . . or a right-hand turn.

From downtown: north on Peachtree, R at fork of Peachtree and West Peachtree.

Along the way, at Peachtree and Third streets, you'll pass Atlanta's fabulous Fox Theatre, one of the country's great movie palaces, with marvelous Moorish architecture, opulent 1920s interiors, and a ceiling full of twinkling stars. It's open now for regular tours: call 881-1977. A bit farther on, at Peachtree and Tenth streets, is a colorful area known as "Tight Squeeze"—so called because, back in our brawling frontier days, riders traveling north out of the city were regularly set upon by bandits lurking in the forests hereabouts, and it was a tight squeeze getting through with your money . . . and your life. In the 1960s, this area was home of Atlanta's vivid hippie colony and now houses small neighborhood shops and businesses. Along this stretch of Peachtree, too, are some of the city's largest and most elegant antique shops and galleries.

Farther out, at the right-hand corner of Peachtree and Fourteenth streets, is the futuristic micropolis of Colony Square, a fascinating small urban environment of offices, town houses, shops and restaurants, and the dazzling Colony Square Hotel. Just behind Colony Square to the right, wandering a maze of tree-lined streets, is Ansley Park, a fine old residential area dating to the early 1900s. Before the midtown boom, Ansley Park had slid into decay, but now it is the site of some of the city's most interesting and beautiful restorations. Young Atlanta architects and designers, as well as some of her younger and more innovative politicians and civic leaders, live here in immaculately restored old town houses, along with a sprinkling of Atlanta's wealthiest old families.

Across the street from Colony Square, on your left, is the Atlanta Memorial Arts Center. Here, in this one white building which serves as a memorial to 122 Atlantans who were killed in a Paris air crash while on a cultural tour in 1962, are housed the excellent High Museum of Art, the Atlanta Symphony, the Atlanta School of Art, and the Alliance Theatre and Studio Theatre. The High Museum has an especially fine Junior Gallery, especially for children.

Drive through Ansley Park: R 15th, L Peachtree Circle, R Westminster, L The Prado, L 17th St., L Inman Circle, L Peachtree Circle, R Peachtree, continue on Peachtree about 3 miles to Peachtree Battle, L Peachtree Battle, R Habersham, R Cherokee, L Andrews, R into gates of Atlanta Historical Society—if closed, continue ½ block to West Paces.

The Atlanta Historical Society is housed in a spectacular new headquarters building set back in the eighteen wooded acres crowning the hill. It preserves the best of Georgia's past in art, artifacts, and exhibits. Also on the grounds is the Swan House, a fine Palladian villa set on the very crest of the hill, also open for tours; the Tullie Smith House, a perfectly restored Georgia farmhouse of the 1840s, is here too, as is the Swan Coach House, formerly the carriage and servants' quarters for the Swan House, now an elegant small restaurant and gift shop.

Go out the rear gates of the Swan House, L Slaton, L West Paces Ferry.

This drive will take you through some of the finest of the stately old homes that have given to Atlanta's Northwest the distinction of being called the most beautiful residential area in the country. On your right on West Paces Ferry—named for a gentleman called Benjamin Pace, who once operated a ferry at the road's end, where it crosses the Chattahoochee River—is the Cherokee Town Club, once a fine old home and now a private club. About three blocks farther, on the right, is the new Georgia Governor's Mansion, a Greek Revival mansion atop a beautifully planted rise. Georgia decorators have furnished it with authentic Georgia Federal antiques, and it's a favorite place for Atlantans to take out-of-town visitors on appointed days. Call first. After seeing the mansion, relax for a lovely residential driving tour along winding streets lined with columned old houses set far back on sweeping green lawns.

From West Paces Ferry, just past mansion: R Tux-edo, R at fork, L Blackland, L Northside, L Valley, R Habersham, R West Paces Ferry, L I-75 South. Exit Courtland, 5 blocks, L Auburn, L Hogue just past Dr. King home, L Irwin, R Boulevard.

As you exit on Courtland, you'll see the spires of the new Atlanta Center Limited, another of our fast-rising total urban complexes, with shops, offices, restaurants, and the new Atlanta Hilton Hotel. When you turn onto Auburn Avenue, you'll be on a street of totally black-owned businesses, one of the first in the nation. Since the turn of the century, Auburn has been a thriving commercial center and is one of the main arteries carrying the lifeblood of the city. On this street also is the headquarters for the Southern Christian Leadership Conference, founded by Atlanta's native son and Nobel Peace Prize winner, Dr. Martin Luther King, Jr. Three blocks on Auburn from Courtland is the Ebenezer Baptist Church, where Dr. King shared the pulpit with his father, Atlanta's beloved "Daddy King." Adjacent to the church is Dr. King, Jr.'s gravesite and memorial, where an eternal flame now burns to the memory of this remarkable man. Across the street is the Dr. King, Jr., Community Center, and one block farther on Auburn is Dr. King's birthplace, now open to the public.

L Rt. 485, in middle of bridge, L fork to I-75/I-85 South, exit MLK Blvd. about 1½ miles, L Washing-ton (one block), L Mitchell, L Memorial, L MLK Blvd.

You're now in the Tri-Governmental complex of Atlanta, one of the very few such complexes in the United States. As you exit MLK Boulevard, you'll see the Georgia State Capitol, its dome gilded with real gold panned in the North Georgia mountains, where one of the country's first gold rushes took place. Notice the Capitol grounds: there's something lovely blooming there at every season of the year. On your left as you exit is the Georgia Archives Building, a large, windowless monolith quarried of Georgia marble, as are many of the buildings in the Tri-

Governmental complex. Here, in art, artifacts, and records, Georgia's history lives. Its daily tours are pure fascination. Also in the area is the Atlanta City Hall, corner of Washington and Mitchell, and the historic old Immaculate Conception Church, corner MLK Boulevard and Central. The church stands where the original Catholic church stood during Sherman's march into Atlanta; the church's first pastor, Father O'Reilly, is credited with persuading the general to spare Atlanta's churches. You can see a plaque in memory of Father O'Reilly on the grounds of City Hall. Across from Immaculate Conception Church is the entrance to Underground Atlanta, our incredible "city beneath the city," where the shops, saloons, cafés, cobblestones, and gaslights of our brawling young railroad days have been lovingly restored and augmented with exhibits and attractions to form one of the world's truly unique visitor attractions. If you've time for only one stop, perhaps this should be it.

R Central, 1 block from Capitol, L Decatur—Decatur becomes Marietta.

On your right at Central and Decatur is booming, urbane Georgia State University. Also, this is the area of the city called Five Points, the inner heart of the city and financial district for over a century. Here are such Atlanta institutions as the First National Bank, C&S Bank, Trust Company of Georgia, the National Bank of Georgia, Fulton Federal Savings & Loan, and many other savings and loan institutions. At the intersection of Forsyth and Marietta streets stands the statue of Henry Grady, one of the city's great statesmen and newspaper editors, who, after the Civil War, coined the phrase "Atlanta: a city too busy to hate."

Now, because of one-way streets, we will take you around the block, R Spring, R Walton, R Forsyth, R MLK Blvd., cross bridge, R Techwood.

You'll be passing Rich's Department Store, far more than just a fashion pace setter, though it's that, too. The love affair between Atlanta and Rich's is legendary; if a store can be said to embody the spirit of a city, Rich's does so for Atlanta. As you turn onto Techwood Avenue, the incredible Omni International Atlanta complex lies to your left. Here a futuristic sports arena is home to the Atlanta Flames hockey team and the Atlanta Hawks basketball team. The Omni International Hotel offers some five hundred rooms; eight restaurants and six movie houses dine and entertain visitors. Many levels of shopping and luxury boutiques tempt all comers, and a huge ice-skating rink lures kids of all ages.

Continue on Techwood 1 block, L Marietta, R International Blvd., L Spring, R Harris, R Courtland, R International, R Peachtree.

You've just circled Peachtree Center, the urban center that changed the face of Atlanta once and for all. Here, in this series of interconnecting buildings and plazas, architect John Portman has assembled the innovative Hyatt Regency Atlanta Hotel and the soaring, 70-story Peachtree Plaza Hotel, a great merchandise mart, offices, restaurants, an incredibly beautiful shopping mall, a dinner theatre without peer, lushly planted arcades and malls and open spaces with pedestrian seating, and some of the most exciting outdoor sculpture in the world.

During your drive, you'll have seen Atlanta as it was and is; this is Atlanta as it ultimately will be, an Atlanta the entire world is emulating now. You might want to top off your driving tour with a cool drink atop the Hyatt Regency, in the revolving Polaris Lounge, or atop the Peachtree Center Plaza. From seventy stories up, the city is at your feet; it's a fine feeling indeed.

ATLANTA BELLE ÉPOQUE
(*4 hours or more*)

She started as a lusty country girl with, perhaps, a touch of red dirt on her face, but there's always been a natural grace and elegance to Atlanta, an elegance that came to full flower in the languid, dreaming days after the Reconstruction. And though she's an international lady now, the elegance of Atlanta remains. Here's the loveliest of Atlanta, then and now.

Go north on Peachtree Street just beyond 15th Street and park on left for the Atlanta Memorial Arts Center. From outlying areas, I-75 or I-85 South, exit 10th Street, L 10th, L Peachtree to just beyond 15th Street into art-center parking area.

The graceful white Atlanta Memorial Arts Center houses visual and performing arts under one roof. Here's Symphony Hall; the Alliance Theatre, presenting both traditional and experimental theatre; the fine High Museum of Art and the enchanting Junior Gallery; the Atlanta School of Art. Browse to your heart's content. From the museum, take a driving tour of Atlanta's Northwest, one of the most beautiful residential areas in the United States.

From the Arts Center, proceed north on Peachtree about 3 miles, L Peachtree Battle, R Habersham, L West Paces Ferry, R into grounds of the Georgia Governor's Mansion if it's open on the day you choose. The patrolman at the gate will tell you when it is and isn't.

The Georgia Governor's Mansion, a beautiful Greek Revival structure, has been filled with Georgia antiques from the Federal period by Georgia designers and is an antique-lover's paradise. The mansion is surrounded by extensive and lovely formal gardens.

L out of gates on West Paces Ferry 1 block, R Tuxedo, R at fork, L Blackland, L Northside, L Valley, R West Paces Ferry, L Andrews, L into the Atlanta Historical Society grounds.

You might easily spend the better part of a day or an afternoon in the grounds of the lovely Atlanta Historical Society. Visit the beautiful Swan House, a Palladian villa built in the 1920s, filled with antiques and accessories from all over the world. Then tour the Tullie Smith House, a lovingly restored Georgia farmhouse of the early 1800s, nestled in the wooded grounds. The restoration included several of the plantation's small outbuildings. There's a fine small craft shop here, featuring handmade items.

You'll want to visit the Swan Coach House, too, which was originally the carriage house and servants' quarters for the Swan House when it was a private residence. An excellent small art gallery is housed here, as well as a charming boutique, and the restaurant has long been a luncheon favorite for Atlanta women.

Star in the crown of the 18-acre Historical Society complex is the new Atlanta Archives Building, with a priceless collection of arts, artifacts, and exhibits. Georgia's vivid history comes alive here. There is a film presentation which changes periodically.

Also fun and convenient for lunch, if you're not lunching at the Coach House, are New Orleans' famous Brennan's and the small, charming E.J.'s, nearby.

From the Historical Society grounds, drive out the back gate, turn L on Slaton, R on West Paces Ferry, L into Brennan's 2 blocks away; for E.J.'s: L on Slaton, and straight beyond the light.

If you're inclined toward some intriguing shopping and browsing, continue west from the Historical Society across West Paces Ferry and straight, where you'll find two delightful boutique centers on your right. First is Cates Center, an informal little cluster of clothing, craft, and antique shops built on two levels around an open brick patio. A bit farther along is Andrews Square, an elegant and somewhat larger complex built on two levels around an enclosed courtyard with a splashing fountain. Here are fine specialty shops, jewelry and antiques, boutiques of all sorts.

To go back downtown, take West Paces Ferry to I-75. For downtown, take I-75 South; to go to the Perimeter, I-285 take I-75 North.

We hope you liked our elegant face. It's just one of the many faces of Atlanta.

ALL IN THE FAMILY
(8 hours)

This is a day for the entire family to savor and remember. It takes you from a morning of serenity and reflection on the grounds of a Trappist monastery to a trip through Atlanta's turbulent Civil War days to a stroll through one of the country's outstanding zoos to a visit to Atlanta as she lived and played a century ago—underneath the streets of today's Atlanta. It's peaceful enough for the older generation, vivid and amusing enough for the most discriminating toddler. Go alone if you must, but you'll have more fun when it's all in the family.

From downtown, take I-20 East (about 27 miles) to Ga. 138 exit, R 5 miles to Ga. 212, L 2 miles.

The Monastery of the Holy Ghost was built entirely by the labor and love of the Trappist monks. The abbey itself is a soaring Gothic building; the grounds are spectacular. Women are not permitted in the cloister itself, but men are welcome. Everyone may visit the greenhouse complex, where intricate displays of cactus and bonsai are featured, and a small, fine gift shop offers strong, simple, and lovely pottery and artifacts handmade by the brothers, and loaves of bread produced, milled, and baked on the premises; proceeds go for upkeep and maintenance of the monastery and the few needs of the brothers. A slide presentation shows women the interior and daily life of the community. The tranquil green grounds are a fine place to picnic, if you'd like to pack a lunch.

To Cyclorama: return to I-20 West, exit Boulevard, L Boulevard, R Berne into Grant Park, follow signs to Cyclorama.

Atlanta's famous Cyclorama is considered to be the largest painting in the world and depicts, in three-dimensional, circular fashion, the Battle of Atlanta. It was painted in 1885–86 by a group of German artists commissioned especially for the purpose, and measures fifty feet in height and four hundred feet in circumference. A stirring musical accompaniment and spoken commentary brings the fateful battle alive for present-day pilgrims. Downstairs in the same building is the Texas, the locomotive that pursued and caught the locomotive General in the daring Andrews Raid, in 1862—a chase so vivid that it became the subject of the movie *The Great Locomotive Chase*.

Just a short distance away in Grant Park is the Atlanta Zoological Park—the zoo, as generations of young Atlantans have called it. Atlanta's zoo can claim one of the country's finest reptile houses, a fine children's zoo, and the world's largest collection of crocodiles, housed in solariums on either end of the reptile building. The zoo is home to a host of exotic animals; be sure to drop by to see Willie B., the lowland gorilla who lords it over the primate house. He's named for one of Atlanta's most beloved mayors, William B. Hartsfield, and is almost as famous locally as Hizzoner was. The shady grounds around Grant Park's lake are fine for picnicking, too, and there are ample snack and short-order places in the park.

To Underground Atlanta: return to I-20 West, exit Capitol Avenue, R MLK Blvd. to Underground Atlanta Parking.

Underground Atlanta today looks much as Atlanta did in the colorful, brawling days before and during the Civil War, when the burgeoning young railroads set the tenor and flavor of the city. Here are the shops, saloons, warehouses, and cafés, the cobblestones and gaslights that served the young town, meticulously restored to their former glory . . . and then some. As the city grew, a network of bridges and viaducts gradually spanned the old section, until it literally sank underground and was forgotten for generations, except to the city's derelicts and an occasional adventuresome native. Many of the original storefronts and old signs are here, shining new again, and many cafés, restaurants, museums, and other attractions have been added just for fun. There are several places to have a meal, with foods from all over the world, from fine French to the nickel lunch of a century ago; music reverberates down the cobbled streets; nightclubs offer a wide variety of entertainment, and the whole complex is fascinating for an hour, an afternoon, or a whole evening. Youngsters especially will enjoy the musical museum, with more than three hundred musical instruments in good working order, and the Underground Wax Museum, where more than one hundred historical and literary personages from all eras of history seem to live again. From JFK to Martin Luther King to Henry VIII to Count Dracula. . . .

It's a dizzying trip, but great fun. Have a late snack in one of the many restaurants; you've definitely earned it.

STONE MOUNTAIN SOJOURN
(5 to 7 hours)

This day in the country takes you to the family wonderland that encompasses Stone Mountain, the largest outcropping of exposed granite in the world. The 3,200-acre park surrounding it contains so much to do and see that you'll want to give yourself ample time. Besides the wealth of recreational facilities, much of the park focuses on the Old South and features museums, exhibits, restorations, concerts, and scheduled special events. The mountain is more than 200 million years old, and the legends and customs that have gathered around its massive gray shoulders are legion. Generations of Atlantans have climbed it, by sunlight and moonlight; you'll want to take it all in. Then you'll have time for a leisurely browse through the charming little boutiques in nearby Stone Mountain Village. It's a full day but an unforgettable one. Wear walking or climbing shoes; sneakers are preferable.

From downtown take I-85 South, exit I-20 East, exit I-285 Chattanooga, exit Stone Mountain Freeway— Athens, exit Stone Mountain Park, enter park (about 17 miles from downtown).

You might start your tour at Memorial Hall, the best place to view Stone Mountain's famous equestrian carvings of Jefferson Davis, Robert E. Lee, and Stonewall Jackson. These great carvings, the world's largest, were begun in 1923 by the sculptor of Mount Rushmore, Gutzon Borglum. Recently completed, they cover an area the size of a football field.

Faithful to the theme of the Old South is the antebellum plantation complex, with nineteen authentically restored buildings. There is a Civil War museum, an antique auto museum, an around-the-mountain ride in replicas of the Civil War locomotives General and Texas, paddle-wheel steamer excursions on huge Stone Mountain Lake, a grist mill, sorghum mill, cider press, and authentic covered bridge.

Especially fun for kids is the see-and-touch game ranch, also the Swiss skylift to the top of the mountain, where, from the top of Mountaintop Tower, you can indeed see practically forever on a clear day.

Stone Mountain's 732-bell carillon is featured in scheduled concerts, and its sweet voice singing out over the lake is a once-in-a-lifetime experience. The park's marina, on the lake, is one of the largest boat rentals in the country. Rowboats, canoes, even whaleboats—all will take you out for fine fishing or a scenic tour of the lovely lake. There's great swimming from four sand beaches in the summertime, too.

For sports enthusiasts, there's an 18-hole championship golf course, horseback riding, hiking and climbing trails, campgrounds. And a sound-and-light re-enactment of Sherman's March to the Sea will please everybody.

Taste it all, of course, but don't let the planned attractions overshadow the incredible natural beauty of the park. Dogwood and flowers are spectacular in spring and summer, fall foliage on the dense hardwoods equally so. Get to know the small, enchanting, out-of-the-way nooks and crannies of the park. They're lovely places to pause and rest and picnic.

For lunch, try the southern buffet at the Stone Mountain Inn; it's really fine. The Plantation Restaurant is a shade more formal. Picnics at Stone Mountain are traditional, too.

From the west gate of Stone Mountain Memorial Park, drive just a few miles to charming little Stone Mountain Village, where some of the area's most intriguing shopping hides away in amusing, well-restored small structures.

Exit West Gate, continue straight, L at Main Street (traffic light), R just past old train station to park.

Try Calico Junction for handcrafts and gifts, Wells Cargo for crafts, the Flower Box for gifts and floral arrangements, Memory Lane for antiques. There are several other antique shops here, and the Glass Works has beautiful creations in stained glass, plus a chance to watch artisans at work. The Gingerbread House is home to several intriguing boutiques, a unique little Christmas shop among them. There are others. Wander and look.

And then, back downtown. We *told* you it was a full day, didn't we?

L out of parking on Main St., L Memorial Drive at light to Rte. 78 to Atlanta, exit I-285, L to I-20 Birmingham, exit I-20 Birmingham, exit I-75/I-85, exit International for downtown.

SHERMAN'S MARCH
(8 hours or more)

General Sherman's ascent from Kennesaw Mountain to Peachtree Creek was inexorable once "Old Joe" Johnston was forced to retreat from the mountain. Weary of Johnston's desperate retreating, Atlanta cried for replacement. And after Johnston was forced back across the Chattahoochee River, General Hood, one of his corps commanders and an impulsive, aggressive tactician, took his place. He attacked at Peachtree Creek, Decatur, Ezra Church. The attacks failed. Within the month, Atlanta was under siege. In November 1864, Sherman put the city to the torch and rode out of the blackened rubble toward Savannah and the sea. As nearly as modern roads and highways permit, this tour tracks Sherman's march from Kennesaw through Atlanta.

Drive north on I-75, exit Kennesaw Mountain exit, about 5 miles past I-285, L Cobb Pkwy., R 41, L on Rte. 3, 2 miles, follow signs to Kennesaw Mountain Battlefield Park.

At the Visitor Center of Kennesaw Mountain National Battlefield Park, museum exhibits and a good fifteen-minute film depict the history of the Atlanta campaign. A short drive takes you almost to the summit of Kennesaw Mountain, and a climbing trail from the parking area winds to the very top of the mountain, where you can look twenty-two miles east to today's Atlanta . . . and pause to reflect how it must have looked in 1864 to the tired men who wore blue and gray. Gun emplacements and exhibits along the way trace the action in more detail.

Cheatham Hill, site of one of the mountain's fiercest battles, lies about five miles south of the Visitor Center on well-marked roads. Here a walking trail winds among existing gun emplacements and Confederate earthworks. There are pleasant picnic grounds here, too.

Also nearby on well-marked roads is the Kolb farm, a restored Civil War structure that saw a particularly bloody afternoon's fighting. Southern forces suffered extremely heavy losses here.

Throughout the battlefield area there are several hiking trails of varying distances. Some are quite steep and long, but well worth the effort. A gallant and bloody page of Atlanta's history was written here, and in these quiet fields the men of both armies don't seem far away.

Next, a short trip to the nearby Big Shanty Museum, to see the General, made famous by the movie *The Great Locomotive Chase*. (This occurred in 1862, well before General Sherman came calling, but should not be missed.)

To Big Shanty: return to 41, north about 2 miles, R Rte. 293, go about 2 miles to Cherokee and museum.

The General was captured from Big Shanty (now Kennesaw) in April 1862 by the daring Andrews Raiders. It was pursued by Confederate Captain William Fuller in the locomotive Texas in a wild, cliff-hanging and ultimately successful rescue attempt. The General survived the war and served in private duty until it finally came to rest in Chattanooga, staying on display there many years, when the L&N Railroad decided to bring it home to Kennesaw. But Chattanooga citizens seized the engine, and a three-year court battle ensued. The Supreme Court finally awarded it to the L&N, and the General came home at last to Big Shanty, where it stands now in its own museum, a carefully restored cotton gin. The museum houses the General and its tender, exhibits, and a narrated slide film of Andrews' raid.

Driving about eight miles south on Rte. 41, you'll come to Paces Mill Road. Take a right, and in a short while you'll be in the charming old village of Vinings, a settlement clustered at the base of Vinings Mountain, another of General Sherman's premier Atlanta-watching vantage points. You may want to have lunch at the Paces Tea Room, a fine old home now serving delightful luncheons in a beguiling setting. After lunch, take time to stroll through the cluster of antique and gift shops and boutiques in Vinings village; most are housed in restored old white frame houses out of another era, and their wares are exceptionally good. Then drive up to the top of Vinings Mountain and see for yourself what General Sherman saw on his way east for an appointment downtown.

From Vinings village follow West Paces Ferry Road to Peachtree Road, R Peachtree to Collier, R Collier a short distance to park on L.

The Battle of Peachtree Creek was a decisive one in the ultimate fall of Atlanta. Here General Hood brashly engaged General Sherman at his encampment. Vastly outnumbered, the Confederates were forced to fall back into the city itself, and for the first time, Atlanta citizens saw their bloody and defeated army come straggling into town past their homes. After Peachtree Creek, war was in Atlanta proper. Here in this quiet spot on Collier Road, an open-air visitors center with self-guiding markers and a map commemorates this fateful arena.

From the memorial park, continue on Collier, L Northside, R onto I-75 South, exit I-20 East, exit Boulevard, R Boulevard, R Berne, follow signs to the Cyclorama.

The last chapter in today's story is the world-famous Cyclorama of the Battle of Atlanta, housed in its own building in Grant Park. It was painted in 1885–86 by a group of German artists brought to America expressly for the purpose and measures fifty feet in height and four hundred feet in circumference. Stirring musical accompaniment and historical commentary combine with the great three-dimensional painting itself to bring the Battle of Atlanta chillingly to life.

Also in the Cyclorama building is the Texas, the pursuing locomotive in *The Great Locomotive Chase*. Fort Walker, nearby on well-marked roads in the park, was one of the central city's prime fortifications and still retains many of its cannon and trenches. There's a heart-lifting view of the city from the fort's vantage point.

If you're not out of steam, do stroll through Atlanta's fine zoo, also nearby, within Grant Park. The reptile house and the children's zoo are especially good.

Otherwise, back downtown . . . and back into today.

L Berne, L Boulevard, L I-20 West, R I-75/I-85 North, for downtown Atlanta.

ATLANTA'S BLACK HERITAGE
(*3 to 6 hours*)

Perhaps no city in America has been so strengthened, vitalized, and enriched by its black community, past and present, as has Atlanta. From ante-bellum days to now, black men and women of extraordinary vision and grit have given to Atlanta priceless gifts in the areas of education, business and industry, civic and cultural leadership, political guidance, and social change. This tour is designed to acquaint you with Atlanta's black community as it is today, and with the roots, inalterably intertwined with those of the city at large, that gave it life.

And, as a bonus, there's a loving look at a once-proud neighborhood that's glowing into spectacular new life.

From downtown take I-85 South, exit I-20 West, exit Ashby, L Ashby, R Oglethorpe—a short block past MLK Blvd., R Peeples, L Ashby, continue I-20 West; or if you wish, stop at Wren's Nest from Peeples, L MLK Blvd., about a block to Wren's Nest on left. Return to MLK Blvd., to Ashby, L to I-20 West.

Peeples Street is the heart of Atlanta's fabled West End district, which flourished as an area of great old Victorian homes at the end of the nineteenth century, slid into gentle decay as the city moved eastward, and is blooming again in all its former glory, thanks to the love, energy, and dedication of a young local architect. In co-operation with the city, the gas and electric companies, many private citizens, and the American Institute of Architects, young Wade Burns is redeveloping West End into the enchanting, authentic neighborhood of gaslights, brick sidewalks and arches, and pristine, century-old houses it once was. Many of the most luminous names in the city's history have their roots here, including former Secretary of State Dean Rusk, and it's a fascinating half hour or so to see these streets and houses emerging again from their long sleep. If there's time, do take a short detour to the Wren's Nest, home of Atlanta's beloved Joel Chandler Harris, who created the wonderful Uncle Remus stories. Here still is the mailbox where a mother wren raised her family during Harris's time and so named the old house. Much Harris memorabilia is still in the house, and on the grounds you can see "Thimblefinger Well," "Snap Bean Farm," and the infamous "Briar Patch."

Continue I-20 West, exit Hightower North, R Hightower, L Collier, R Waterford, R Aline, R Peek, L Laverne, L Aline, L Waterford, R Collier, L Linkwood, R MLK Blvd., L Lynhurst, R Mangum, L Braemer, L

Oakcrest, R Clearbrook, R Kingsdale, R Cascade, R I-285 North, R I-20 East, to Atlanta.

The area you're driving through now is called Collier Heights, and many of Atlanta's most influential black families live here. This area was developed shortly after World War II by a black contractor exclusively for black owners and has remained one of the most stable and attractive neighborhoods in Atlanta's west side. On Aline Road, notice the mule wagon and freedom bell.

Cascade Heights, the next residential area, dates its history back at least fifty years and is, perhaps, to the west side what Buckhead is to Atlanta's north side. These quiet, winding, tree-shaded streets are studded with homes ranging from the frankly opulent to the modest; their owners range from a mayor and a newspaper publisher and a baseball star to mechanics and postal workers. Cascade Heights is today, as it always has been, an ultimate experience in sharing—of homes, of lifestyles, of aspirations, and of a long black heritage.

From I-20 East exit Windsor-Spring, L Spring about 1 mile, L MLK Blvd., R Sunset, L Simpson, L Chestnut, L MLK Blvd., R Tatnall, R Walnut, L Fair, R Northside, R Spelman, L Greens Ferry, R Chestnut, L Fair, L Ashby, L I-20 East.

As you turn on Sunset, you are on the street where Dr. Martin Luther King, Jr., lived at the time of his death. On Chestnut Street you'll see the John F. Kennedy Middle School and Community Center, designed in 1970 by world-renowned Atlanta architect John Portman, whose soaring Peachtree Center changed the face of Atlanta. This unique complex houses, in addition to its middle school, facilities for senior-citizen activities and adult education, a child day-care center, programs for the mentally retarded, counseling and legal services, and a prekindergarten program. If you've time, students will take you on a tour of this dynamic complex.

If you are hungry and wish to have lunch before continuing on your tour of the Atlanta University complex, take a right on Dr. Martin Luther King Boulevard, after Chestnut, rather than a left, and continue to Pascal's Motel, at 830 Dr. Martin Luther King Boulevard, then return and continue your tour. You won't want to miss Pascal's. This nationally acclaimed restaurant is part of a complex including a motor hotel that has been called home of the finest black-owned hotel facility in the country, and the motel's La Carrousel Lounge is also home of the greatest names in jazz whenever they're in town. Do check to see who's playing while you are there.

You're on the fringes of one of the world's greatest and most unique university complexes. Atlanta University Center began life more than a century ago in a box car. Today, it's one of the most outstanding centers for black education in the world. The University Center comprises six colleges, all sharing facilities, faculty, and students, yet each remaining autonomous. In the order of the route you're driving, they are Morris Brown; the Interdenominational Theological Center; Spelman College, with its exquisite Sisters Chapel; Atlanta University, with one of the country's great collections of black art; Clark College; and Morehouse College, Alma Mater of Dr. Martin Luther King, Jr. If you have time, stop at the Atlanta University library and wander these quiet, beautiful, tree-shaded campuses. They're serene islands in a sea of commerce.

Exit I-75/I-85 North, exit International Blvd., L Courtland 3 blocks to L Auburn, L Hogue, L Irwin, R Boulevard, L Rte. 485, right-lane, exit International.

Auburn Avenue, known fondly as "Sweet Auburn," is a street of totally black-owned businesses, one of the nation's first. Since the turn of the century, Auburn Avenue has been one of Atlanta's most affluent commercial centers. Four blocks on Auburn, off Courtland Street, is the Ebenezer Baptist Church, where Atlanta's beloved Nobel Prize winner, Dr. Martin Luther King, Jr. shared the pulpit with his father, "Daddy King." Adjacent to the church is Dr. King, Jr.'s gravesite, where an eternal flame now burns to his memory. One block farther down is the birthplace of Dr. King, Jr. Plan on visiting the church, the Dr. Martin Luther King, Jr., Center, and his birthplace. Headquarters for the Southern Christian Leadership Conference is also on Auburn Avenue.

This tour will give you a taste of a luminous heritage impossible to duplicate anywhere.

A KID'S-EYE VIEW

There is so much to do in Atlanta that will intrigue children. They can be safely included in most of the daytime tours in this book and many of the nighttime tours. The following four, however, have been especially child-tested and approved . . . which certainly does not mean that the accompanying adults won't have a glorious time, too. Here's a child's-eye view of Atlanta's exhilarating downtown; a visit with Uncle Remus, Rosebud the Cow, and Rodin; a day spent at the wonderland that is Six Flags over Georgia, and another day spent in the heart of darkest Africa—less than an hour away from downtown. Grab a kid or two or three and go . . . but don't be ashamed if someone catches you sneaking off on these tours sans kids; it happens all the time.

DOWNTOWN: BIG STUFF FOR SMALL FRY
(6 to 8 hours)

If you ever doubted that a big city's downtown section is a country of inklings, oddments, and enchantments, see it with a child in tow. Young eyes have a way of seeing wonders that older ones have grown blind to, and Atlanta's downtown is especially rich in sights, sounds, and textures. Grab your sneakers and your offspring, or borrow someone else's, and off you go.

Take I-85/I-75 South from downtown (or North if staying south of town), exit I-20 East, exit Boulevard, R Boulevard, R Berne into Grant Park and Cyclorama.

Atlanta's unique Cyclorama is said to be the world's largest painting, and depicts the Battle of Atlanta in circular, three-dimensional form. It measures fifty feet in height and four hundred feet in circumference, and was painted in the mid-1880s by a group of talented German artists imported especially for the purpose. Generations of Atlanta children have watched history come vividly alive as they stood in the center of this stirring exhibit, listening to a clear, simple recorded commentary and spine-tingling music and absorbing the spectacle that changed the course of the city's destiny. Downstairs in the Cyclorama building is the locomotive Texas, which pursued and caught the engine General in the daring Andrews Raid of 1862. Your kids will love seeing the real star of the movie *The Great Locomotive Chase.*

While you're in Grant Park, do stroll through Atlanta's excellent zoo, which is also there. Signs will direct you from the Cyclorama building. The zoo contains what is considered to be one of the best reptile houses in the country, a first-rate children's zoo with pettable small creatures, and a generally good collection of exotic and domestic animals, including the famed gorilla Willie B., named (affectionately) for one of Atlanta's most beloved mayors, the late William B. Hartsfield. Then, a very short detour for historic Fort Walker.

To get to Fort Walker, return to Boulevard, R on Boulevard, follow signs.

Fort Walker, at Grant Park's highest point, was one of the city's central fortifications during the fateful Battle of Atlanta. The trenches and cannon are still there, in fine shape, and there's a 200-foot observation tower on the grounds which gives you a stunning view of the city skyline to the northwest.

From Fort Walker, return to I-20 via Boulevard, L I-20 West, exit Capitol Avenue (2nd exit) for the Archives Building.

The Georgia Department of Archives Building, just across the way from the State Capitol, is considered to be one of the most advanced archives buildings in the world. Special tours highlighting the science of protecting old documents can be arranged with the tour guide daily in the mornings and afternoons. Another favorite with the children is "The Rise and Fall of the Confederacy," a stunning panorama done in stained-glass windows commissioned by Mr. Amos G. Rhodes for his home at the turn of the century and moved from the old Rhodes home on

Peachtree Street to the archives building. Framed by a Honduran-mahogany staircase and lit as they were in the old Rhodes home, they are overwhelming. The vestibule of the archives building contains a wealth of displays and artifacts from Georgia's past and present.

To Capitol, follow Capitol Avenue, runs into MLK Blvd., park for State Capitol Building.

Georgia's State Capitol Building is the nucleus of Atlanta's Tri-Governmental complex, one of the very few such complexes in the nation. Here the business of the state, county, and city goes on in a series of integrated marble and granite buildings. The dome of the statehouse is gilded with real gold, brought from Dahlonega, in the North Georgia mountains, where one of the country's very first gold rushes took place. Georgia's most famous native sons are commemorated throughout the Capitol in busts, and famous southerners adorn the lawns in statuary—a favorite sight for kids and pigeons. The fourth-floor museum of state resources, products, and events is especially good for youngsters, and a glimpse at the Georgia legislature in session can be one of the greatest shows on earth. The General Assembly convenes in January and February; ask for passes to the House at the speaker's office and the Senate at the lieutenant governor's office. If there's time, the guided building tours are fun and free. Ask at the information desk in the lobby and on the second floor.

Follow MLK Blvd. (one way), R Spring, about 2 miles, L North Avenue into Varsity.

You've had a morning in Georgia's past. Have some lunch now in one of the most legendary and beloved of her present-day landmarks—the Varsity. This double-decker drive-in is the world's largest and was started to serve neighboring Georgia Tech, across the way. Since then, its hot dogs, chili dogs, french-fried onion rings, fried pies, Coca-Colas, and most of all, its wacky, wild waiters and their colorful slang have become world famous. Eat in your car or go inside and watch TV while you dine, but go. It's a hands-down winner with kids.

Directions to the Coca-Cola Building: from parking lot go right on North Avenue 4 blocks to Coca-Cola Building on left.

There's no doubt about it . . . Coca-Cola *is* Atlanta. It was born and bred here, and millions of children all over the world can probably say "Coca-Cola" before they can say "Mama." Your kids will love the charming "Reflections" exhibit in the new, white headquarters building on North Avenue. Here is a truly fascinating collection of Coca-Cola memorabilia, from the very first bottles and trays to the posters and art work that characterized it through the decades. It's a walk through the history of a city, a country, and a soft drink . . . and your next Coke will taste better after you've seen it. (Call first, at 892-4000.)

Go back on North Avenue as you came, L on Techwood—just past Stadium, L 4th Street, R Campus Drive, R on Atlantic, R Feist, L Fowler.

It's formally named the Georgia Institute of Technology, but your kids—and the world—know it as Georgia Tech. Drive through this world-famous downtown campus, past the famous "Tech Tower," which has dominated the midtown skyline for generations, through the streets of "Fraternity Row," past Grant Field, where the Ramblin' Wrecks have become gridiron legend. If there's time, you might want to stop off and see the famed Rich Computer Center or the Neely Nuclear Reactor; any student on campus will point the way.

Directions to Arts Center from Tech campus: R 10th Street, L Peachtree, L into Arts Center parking (between 15th and 16th streets on left).

The High Museum of Art, in the beautiful white Atlanta Memorial Arts Center, has a special junior-activities center which is sure to intrigue your youngsters. Here are child-tailored exhibitions, studio classes, and a special art gallery and shop designed to introduce and cultivate an enduring taste for fine art in children. The museum proper will appeal to older children too, and there are regularly scheduled performances of theatre and symphony for children, many in the afternoons. Call 892-3600 for information.

Directions back downtown. From parking L 15th Street, R Peachtree to downtown Atlanta; for I-85 or I-75, R 15th, L West Peachtree, R 14th Street, 2 blocks to expressway.

SIX FLAGS OVER GEORGIA
(A morning, an afternoon, an evening, or all three)

There's no describing Six Flags over Georgia, except to say that since it opened, in the late 1960s, it's changed the habits of almost every family in Atlanta and many visiting families. Lots of visitors plan an entire vacation around it; the park's claim that it's almost impossible to see and do everything isn't far from wrong. Essentially, Six Flags is a theme amusement park commemorating the six flags that have flown over the state of Georgia since it was born . . . and even before; and there are special rides and exhibits planned around each culture. But that doesn't even begin to give you an idea. So go, do, see, as much as possible, for as long as possible. (Adults in your bunch will enjoy the immaculate, beautifully planted grounds and the charming young people who are hosts and hostesses, even when they're tired out and need a rest. We've never personally known a kid who pooped out.)

I-85/I-75 to I-20 West, exit Six Flags sign (about 12 miles), L into park. From Perimeter (I-285), exit I-20 West, two exits to Six Flags, L, R into Park.

There are more than one hundred rides and attractions at Six Flags. To list them would be futile, but favorites among them are the fabulous Crystal Pistol Music Hall, the Chevy Show, Dodge City, the Phlying Phlurpus, the Civil War Steam Train, the French Riverboat Rides, the Dolphin Show, the Drunken Barrels, the Runaway Mine Train, the Log Flume, the world's highest and longest roller coaster (and scariest, we have on good authority), the Great American Scream Machine, and don't miss the

Great Gasp—a 325-foot parachute jump that lands you on the ground in twenty-eight seconds!

There are countless shows, too, and music everywhere, from strolling street bands to such luminous names as Tony Orlando and Dawn, Helen Reddy, Olivia Newton-John, Gladys Knight and the Pips, and Jose Feliciano. Puppet shows, magic shows, carousels, nighttime fireworks exhibits, and probably more kinds of food at more different places than you could sample in a month of Sundays. Smaller children love the Petting Zoo, and there's a special section for toddlers and tykes, featuring gentler shows and exhibits. The restrooms are ample and spotless. There are plenty of comfortable places to get in out of the rain, and fine first-aid stations and facilities.

Your whole family shouldn't leave Atlanta until you've all seen Six Flags. But if you can't make it, feel no qualms about dropping off older children and telling them to meet you back at the main gate at such-and-such a time. It may be Atlanta's most popular child-meeting place.

THE THREE R'S
(5 to 7 hours)
Remus, Rosebud, and Rodin—it adds up to a fine day grounded in folklore, a real farm, and fine art. If you'd like to picnic, pack a lunch to savor down on the farm. Or, the famous Varsity Drive-In is on your route. This tour is a great favorite with young Atlantans.

From I-85/I-75 take I-20 West, exit Ashby—3rd exit after I-85, L Ashby, R MLK Blvd. to Wren's Nest on left.

The Wren's Nest, the lovely old home of Joel Chandler Harris, creator of the beloved Uncle Remus stories, is a pilgrimage that few Atlanta children have missed. If your kids know the wonderful stories of Br'er Fox, Br'er Rabbit, the Tar Baby, and the other charming Uncle Remus characters, they'll love seeing the graceful old place where they were written. The house takes its name from the mailbox, still to be seen, where a wren built a nest and raised her

young undisturbed during Harris's time. There are many
Harris memorabilia: original furnishings, books, photo-
graphs, personal articles and, on the grounds, "Thimblefinger Well," the "Briar Patch," and "Snap Bean
Farm." You might like to read your young a few of the
stories before the trip; the Atlanta Public Library has
them.

*From Wren's Nest, R MLK Blvd., L Ashby to I-20
East, exit Candler Rd.—about 10 miles, R, L 2nd light,
Rainbow, about ½ mile to Mathis Dairy on right.*

R. L. Mathis Dairy has tours of a real, working dairy
which take your young through a spotless plant (and, for
lagniappe, delivers a chocolate milk drink at the end of
the tour), a charming collection of affable cows, sheep,
rabbits, and ponies who welcome visits, and a chance to
milk Rosebud, who is perhaps Atlanta's most famous and
best-natured cow. A supervised session with Rosebud will
earn your child an "I milked Rosebud" button, and visits
to the milking parlor and the maternity ward are *de rigueur.* There are also beautiful picnic grounds at the dairy
for lunching in fine weather. Call 289-1433 ahead of time
to make sure it's a tour day.

*Directions to the Varsity: Return to Candler Road, L
to I-20 West, exit I-75/I-85 North, exit North Avenue, L
to Varsity.*

If you didn't picnic at the dairy, by all means stop off at
the Varsity, world's largest drive-in. They're famous for
their chili dogs and fried pies and wild and wonderful
waiters, and everything else is good, too.

*From the Varsity, L Spring Street, R 10th, L Peach-
tree, to Memorial Arts Center parking lot, just past
15th Street on left.*

The Atlanta Memorial Arts Center was funded and
built as a memorial to 122 Atlanta art patrons who died in
an air crash in Paris in 1962 while on a cultural tour. To
commemorate this tragic event, the French Government
presented the city with a casting of Auguste Rodin's
magnificent *"L'Ombre"* (The Shade), which now stands

on the steps at the entrance to the High Museum. It's not to be missed. Of special interest to children is the museum's unique Junior Activities Center, featuring special exhibitions, studio classes, and a gallery and art shop just for small fry. Symphony Hall, the Atlanta School of Art, and the Alliance Theatre are all under this soaring white roof, too; a walk around will intrigue everybody. Occasionally, there are special afternoon symphony and theatre performances for children. You might want to call 892-3600 before you take the tour, to find out.

From parking garage of Arts Center: R 15th Street, R Peachtree to downtown; to I-85/I-75: R 15th, L West Peachtree, R 14th, 2 blocks to expressway.

WILD AND WOOLLY
(*4 to 8 hours or more*)

A trip to Atlanta's Kingdoms 3, where wild animals roam free through hundreds of acres of wooded park, could be *the* day of a young naturalist's life. You'll be in your closed car, of course, and trained safari guides will be along the way to protect you if a rhino or an elephant should get rambunctious. But, so far, we've never heard of a case of nerves, animal or human. It's safe, fun, and an absolutely unforgettable experience.

To Kingdoms 3, take I-75 South, exit Hwy. 138, turn R, follow signs.

Your Wild Kingdom "safari" will take you along miles of trail, through five areas representing the continents of North America, Asia, and Africa, where prides of wild lions amble about your car. It is the home of some rare white rhinos; you'll see cheetahs, the world's fastest land animal (their top speed, it's said, is 70 mph); curious giraffes might inspect you; there are some exceedingly large African elephants; meet a gnu or two; and the zebras definitely have the right of way. The animals don't stick strictly to their appointed areas, of course. You're apt to meet any kind anywhere along the way. Then, there are fine flocks of flamingos and other exotic birds, many of whom perform tricks that would put an acrobat to shame; ostriches, hippos, antelope, grizzly bears, buffalo—a wonderful sight to see wild things living together in peace and freedom.

After your safari, there are many attractions at the Fun Kingdom: the Pet Corner, Rainbow Rides such as Mr. Toots, the Kiddy Train, Funky Monkey, the Gyro Whip, the Whizzer of Ahs, and the Boomarang, and many more. There's a restaurant that would make a good lunch stop, and your tribe will want to visit Trader Robbie's Curio Hut. Visit Rainbow Plaza for circus-type acts. Nature Kingdom is the third kingdom. Enjoy miles of nature trails, a learning center, and the kingdom's science center.

Kingdoms 3 is only about twenty miles south of Atlanta's city limits and can be seen in a morning or afternoon, but all day is best. Not bad for an authentic trip covering three continents!

EARTH AND SKY
(3 to 6 hours)
Atlanta's Fernbank Science Center is an experience no child should miss, and no adult, either. A joint venture of the DeKalb community at large, the DeKalb Public School System, and the federal government, Fernbank literally brings the science of the heavens and earth into the reach of the general public, and the result is a true wonder.

To Fernbank Science Center: take Piedmont Rd. north, R Ponce de Leon, follow to just before railroad trestle, and turn L Artwood, R Heaton and follow signs.

Fernbank forest offers one and a half miles of well-kept nature trails, where you and your brood can get acquainted with the well-marked flora of the area—hardwoods, pines, wildflowers, mushrooms, an incredible array of ferns—and perhaps a glimpse of some of the small animals that live here. The 65-acre forest also has an experimental garden featuring native and cultivated plants, and a Braille trail designed for the visually handicapped.

The great planetarium, third largest in the United States,

has regularly scheduled programs that bring the heavens vividly and breath-takingly alive. Set to stirring music, this panoramic saga of the night sky is one of Atlanta's favorite shows.

The observatory, open on Friday nights unless the weather is awful, houses the largest telescope in the southeastern United States. From eclipses to comets to astronauts, the goings and comings in the heavens over Atlanta are a wonder few children will forget.

Fernbank's fine science reference library contains more than seven thousand volumes, along with an excellent collection of current and back scientific periodicals on microfilm.

Hodgson House, on the western edge of the forest, houses one of the largest and most complete museum exhibit departments in the nation. Exhibits prepared by artists, taxidermists, model makers, and draftsmen cover an area of nine thousand square feet, and are a hands-down favorite for Atlanta youngsters. Yours are sure to be enchanted.

In addition, Fernbank has an extremely sophisticated electron microscope laboratory and meteorological laboratory, not generally open to drop-in visitors. But you might inquire if somebody in your gang has a special interest.

Whether you're making a morning, an afternoon, or an evening of it, your kids are sure to enjoy lunch or an early dinner in nearby Emory Village, adjacent to the campus of Emory University. A cluster of small eateries dispense glorious, student-approved pizzas, burgers of all varieties, and other hearty fare. Follow the crowds: a hungry college student invariably knows where the best food is, and your kids will get a kick out of dining with the students. (Everybody does.) It's just a short distance from Fernbank on North Decatur Road.

Et Cetera

There are some fine things for small fry to do that aren't

covered by logical, step-by-step tours. They're sure to enjoy the following:

CHILDREN'S THEATRE thrives during the daylight hours. The Atlanta Children's Theatre, in the Memorial Arts Center, has a show going on several times a week, plus one on Sunday afternoons, in season (892-7607). The charming Vagabond Marionettes have performances in the Studio Theatre of the Memorial Arts Center daily and Sunday, in season (892-2414). And the excellent Academy Children's Theatre, on Roswell Road, has a Saturday matinee in season (261-8550). The above theatres sometimes offer nighttime performances for children. Check the daily papers, or call.

CHILDREN'S CONCERTS abound. The Atlanta Symphony holds children's performances from time to time during school hours. Check the newspapers or call 892-2414 to see when. And the Atlanta Music Club often presents the Atlanta Community Orchestra in special performances for children. Call 873-4071, and they'll tell you where and when. There are other special children's musical events during the year, too; again, watch the papers.

SHOPPING, ANTIQUING, BOUTIQUING

Ask an Atlantan where the best places to shop in the city are and you'll probably get a distressed smile, a helpless shrug, and the gentle question, "What did you have in mind?" Atlanta is the shopping mecca for the entire Southeast, and you can probably get just about anything you *did* have in mind, in any area of the city. Atlanta's shopping is scattered and fragmented throughout the Greater Atlanta area; there's no great Fifth Avenue for fashions, no Chelsea for boutiques, no "Antiques Row."

Rich pockets of treasure are scattered throughout the city. Here, then, are tours designed to help you hit the best of all three worlds in a few hours or days: general shopping, antiquing, and boutiquing. We'll take you to Atlanta's own great fashion houses and department stores (plus the ones that have come to town from New York and Dallas); on a walking-shopping tour of downtown; through the large galleries, and small, charming nooks and crannies that have always housed our city's treasury of antiques; to the best of the small, fascinating boutique centers that are springing up like wildflowers downtown, midtown, and in the fashionable suburbs. We'll follow our tours with selected small shops of all varieties that don't fit into a logical tour at all but are simply too charming and unusual to miss: produce markets, flea markets, serendipitous shops of all kinds.

As we said, there are all kinds of shopping, all over town. Every Atlantan has his own favorites, in all categories. These are ours. Bring walking shoes and money, and enjoy!

DOWNTOWN FOR LOVE AND MONEY
(5 to 8 hours, or shorter in part)
Even though a great deal of the city's best shopping has moved to the glittering malls and little boutiques in the suburbs, Atlanta's downtown area remains the vital heart

for urban treasure hunters. Here are the main enclaves of the city's great stores; the dynamic urban "mini-city" complexes with their lush, world-renowned boutiques; the small and traditional shops that have been beloved of residents for many years. You *can* drive this tour, but we suggest you get out your hardiest walking shoes and walk it. You'd be in and out of garages like a flea on a hot griddle otherwise, and might well miss many of our best small emporiums. Besides, there's no better way to get acquainted with the general downtown area.

Downtown shopping has simply got to start with Rich's. Established in 1867, Rich's Department Store has been inalterably bound up in the fabric, heart, and spirit of the city ever since. Seldom has a commercial emporium been so many things to so many people as Rich's has been to Atlantans. Now a giant, ten-story central store, at the corner of Broad and Marietta streets, in downtown Atlanta (and covering a modest couple of blocks), Rich's has five suburban Atlanta branches and will sell you literally anything you need, from a spool of thread to a set of tires and a lube job to a trip to Europe to *haute couture*. There's a place to get a bite on practically every floor, plus a lovely tearoom that's fully as traditional as the store itself.

Take Spring Street south (from Peachtree Center area) just a few blocks to Rich's, L into parking lot by store, or take Marta "Shoppers Bus."

While you're in the area, stroll over to the incredible Atlanta Omni International and drift through the Omni International Bazaar, where small, intriguing shops offer their wares in a three-tiered, European street-market atmosphere. And then on to the Omni's "Luxury Island," where such names as Hermes, Pucci, Christie Brothers Furriers, Lanvin, and other lustrous brand names reign in splendor. Many other medium- to medium-high-priced retail outlets are within the Omni International Bazaar, too. Make a day of it; there are several unusual restaurants on the premises, offering a wide variety of international foods.

To Omni: leave Rich's through Store for Homes on Spring Street side, turn R and walk three blocks to Marietta, L one block to Omni complex.

Peachtree Street downtown and the streets crossing and paralleling it form the very heart of Atlanta's downtown shopping district. There are literally hundreds of stores, large and small, crammed into this compact area. You should make the short walk from the Omni up to Davison's at 180 Peachtree Street, and window shop. It's a favorite lunchtime stroll for Atlantans who work downtown, and the appointed path for serious shoppers.

Davison's, a division of Macy's, is one of the city's largest department stores and carries a complete line of whatever it is you need to outfit yourself and your life in general. The Corner Shoppe has an especially fine selection of antiques.

From Omni, walk back to Spring Street, turn L, walk the few blocks to International, R International to Peachtree. Davison's and other stores to your R, Peachtree Center to L and across the street.

Also in this area of upper Peachtree, as natives call it, are Regenstein's (209 Peachtree) and J. P. Allen (204 Peachtree) for good women's clothing and accessories, children's clothing, and gifts. And Leon Froshin (230 Peachtree) is fine for women's clothing and specialty items.

A note to gentlemen shoppers: There are good men's stores all over the city. In the general area of Peachtree Street south of Davison's, you'll find Muse's, at 52 Peachtree Street. This store, though small, is as much a tradition with generations of Atlanta men and women as is Rich's. Clothing and accessories from Muse's have been *de rigueur* for Atlanta gentlemen since time out of mind, but there's a fine, if smaller, line of women's clothing, too. And, in addition, there are Parks-Chambers (43 Peachtree), Zachry's (87 Peachtree), and H. Stockton (80 Forsyth Street). Granddaddy of 'em all, Brooks Brothers, resides at 145 Peachtree. William Thourlby, TV's original

Marlboro man, also has an elegant little emporium of men's clothing, at 160 Peachtree.

Peachtree Center, at the corner of Peachtree and International Boulevard, about a block north of Davison's, Atlanta's first and perhaps most famous complete urban environment, has, along with its soaring office towers, hotels, restaurants, theatres, parks and sculpture, walks and indoor gardens, a sybaritic shopping gallery, where you can find some of the most exquisite wares in the city, ranging from moderate to very expensive. Clothing, gifts, books, antiques, crafts, paintings, furniture—whatever you want, it's all here.

BOUTIQUE DAY
(4 to 7 hours)
There are literally hundreds of boutiques in Atlanta. Our favorites, however, seem to cluster in and around Atlanta's chic Buckhead and Northwest sections. This tour helps you sample a morning's worth of everything from andirons to zebra rugs, and takes you from a pre-Civil War settlement to three of the city's newest, smartest, and most complete boutique centers.

North on I-75; about 4 miles north of downtown Atlanta, exit Mt. Paran Road, L one block, R on Rte. 41, at light, L Paces Mill Road to Vinings village.

The railroads built the charming old village of Vinings long before the Civil War, and General Sherman mapped his disastrously successful Atlanta campaign from the top of Vinings Mountain, which drowses over the jumble of neat, white, frame houses at its feet. The old houses have been restored and smartened up with paint, spit, and polish, but it still looks much as it must have in another, gentler era. There's some fine antiquing scattered around the few old streets, in the white houses shielded by lilacs and picket fences and arched with great old trees, and a wide variety of clothing, gift, and craft shops. Shops are scattered, so you'll want to park and walk. It's like strolling through a village at the turn of the century. Shop-

keepers wave, gardeners are at work on glorious flower
beds, sleepy cats sun in the spotless shop windows. Don't
miss the Pavilion House, which was built long ago by the
railroads to serve their crews as a dance hall; and keep the
Paces Tearoom in mind for lunch another day, perhaps—
it's unique. Vinings may look quaint and rural, but the selection of merchandise in the shops is uptown and first-
rate; there's little "jonque" here.

*To Cates Center: from where you parked in Vinings,
turn onto West Paces Ferry Road (at light), continue
for several miles, L East Andrews Drive, ½ block to
Cates Center.*

Cates Center is one of northern Atlanta's newest boutique malls; it sweeps in a two-story horseshoe around a
charming brick courtyard. The shopping arcades are all of
brick too, and are covered, so it's good strolling in any
weather. Little wrought-iron tables and chairs and um-
brellas are set out in the open courtyard for relaxing in
fine weather. Cates is strictly fun and informal, a bit less
expensive than Andrews Square, next door, and houses a
fascinating jumble of interior design and furnishing shops,
gifts of every conceivable variety, good women's clothing
and accessory shops, art shops, men's clothing and furnishings, beauty salons, a metaphysical bookstore, lovely oriental wares, exotic shells, and a little nook that will sell you
a snack and a glass of wine or pack you a bountiful hamper. If a shop seems closed during shopping hours, just rap
on the door; in true European fashion, shopkeepers treat
their customers like old and cherished neighbors rather
than strictly as consumers.

*Continue on Andrews Drive to your right, just
around the curve. On your right is Andrews Square.*

Andrews Square, just around the bend from Cates Center, is little-shop-big-name country. It's frankly luxurious,
with price tags to match, but a truly glorious safari for
people who love luster and *panache*. Andrews is enclosed
under one roof, and its two levels of sybaritic shopping
open four-square around a charming little inner courtyard

centered on a glittering fountain. There are jewelry shops galore—most of them the real thing, but some stunning fakes à la Kenneth Jay Lane—and a number of gift shops featuring items you would *not* send maiden Aunt Minnie back in Iowa. There are beautiful—and expensive— women's clothing, costly custom tennis and sports clothing, and some of the most exquisite handbags on the Atlanta scene. Then, there are shops for contemporary furniture and carpets, hair-styling establishments for both sexes, an elegant gourmet cookware emporium, and the Backstage Boutique, which has a treasure trove of unusual theatrical accouterments. The Little Hart's Restaurant, opening into the courtyard on the ground level, is one of the city's prettiest. Lots more, too; bring a large tote and a fat wallet.

For lunch, you might want to try E.J.'s, in Cates Center, a charming spot operated by beloved Atlanta restaurateur Ed Negri; or retrace Andrews Drive back across West Paces Ferry to the Swan Coach House, in the beautiful grounds of the Atlanta Historical Society. It's on your right on Andrews after you cross West Paces Ferry. It once served as the servants' quarters and carriage house for the lovely Palladian Swan House, also on the Historical Society grounds, and serves elegant little luncheons, as well as housing a fine small-gifts and antique shop of its own. Or, going back up Andrews and turning left on West Paces Ferry, you'll come to Brennan's on your left. New Orleans' legendary Creole cookery has lost nothing on the trip to Atlanta.

To Cates Plaza: from West Paces Ferry, R Peachtree, L Pharr Road, to Cates Plaza on right.

After lunch, dip into yet another Cates—Cates Plaza, on Pharr Road, in Buckhead. (Cates is an old, *old* Atlanta name; you'll see it all over the place.) This is the first of the Buckhead boutique complexes as such, and like its newer neighbor on Andrews Drive, Cates Center, it's a two-level, all-brick horseshoe around plenty of good parking. Here are gift and craft shops of all persuasions. There are an unusual number of handmade gifts and articles of clothing in the little shops here, with emphasis on quilting and kitchen items and children's clothing; a really outstanding ultra-contemporary design shop, a tempting needlework shop, and one of the city's premier health-food shops. Almost every shopkeeper on the double-decker arcade has been here long enough to know the others and their regulars, so an especially neighborly, small-town atmosphere prevails. You'll almost certainly be asked in somewhere to put your feet up and have a cup of coffee or tea. Buckheaders treat Cates Plaza almost like their village center. It's a good place to catch us in our Levi's or tennis togs, picking up a loaf of wheat-germ bread or a hostess gift. Informal and fun—see it all.

STRICTLY UPTOWN
(*A few hours or all day*)
When a truly chic northside Atlanta woman needs a little St. Laurent to perk up her winter wardrobe . . . or could use a Chinese empress's robe circa Ming Dynasty to drift around the house in . . . or fancies one perfect marquise diamond from Tiffany's . . . chances are she won't bother going all the way downtown. She'll have the Rolls brought 'round and say, "Lenox Square and Phipps Plaza, James." These two northside pleasure domes do have moderate-to-lower-priced shops in abundance, but among them you'll find the truly lustrous names in *haute couture* and gems from all over the world—plus enough offbeat, funky little shops to keep you busy a full day, if you choose. Wear walking shoes (handmade Italian, preferably) . . . and your Hermes money belt.

From downtown: north on Peachtree 7 miles; or I-85 North, exit Lenox Road, L 3 miles to Lenox Square; or take a Marta bus north on Peachtree (check with driver for correct bus).

Lenox Square was Atlanta's first large shopping center, and as it has developed over the years, its slogan, "Everything's there at Lenox Square," has become virtually true.

Known affectionately to northsiders as simply "the Square," this multi-level, many-malled complex houses over a hundred retail and professional outlets and some of the most fascinating browsing on earth. You truly don't have to spend a lot of money to have fun at "the Square"; during every season of the year, there's something fun and free in the way of entertainment going on in the central mall, from art shows to concerts to crafts exhibits. Its main department stores are Davison's, Atlanta's beloved Rich's, and a splendid newcomer, Neiman-Marcus. All three are treasure troves of designer names and the *haute*st of *couture*, as well as fine sources of moderately priced anything. Neiman's, especially at Christmas time, offers gifts that all of us love to ogle, even if only a fortunate few of us will ever buy. There's a multitude of specialty clothing shops for men and women, with Yves St. Laurent holding forth at Rive Gauch and Courrèges in a brand-new shop, and other fine designer names scattered around. Men will love Britches of Georgetown, as well as the several time-honored local men's emporiums. Then there are variety stores, women's and men's shoe stores (children's, too), beauty salons, cosmetics, bookstores, jewelry stores, toy and hobby shops, and specialty shops too numerous to mention. You can also rent a car or buy an airline ticket, mail a letter at the Post Office, see a movie or go bowling, see a doctor or dentist, and have a drink, a snack, or a meal at any one of several good restaurants. The Magic Pan serves delectable crepes; El Chico has good Mexican food; and Houlihan's pretty, plant-filled, sky-lit restaurant offers hearty and unusual fare—if you can get in. It's become a lunchtime and after-work mecca for young single Atlantans. Other good quick-food places and cafeterias, too. All in all, Lenox Square is probably the city's largest and most eye-catching mixture of earthy and rarefied shopping. You won't want to miss it.

Drive out of Lenox Square, R Peachtree Road, heading north. Phipps Plaza is about half a block on your left.

When Phipps Plaza was built, in the late 1960s, such glittering names as Tiffany's, Lord & Taylor, Saks Fifth Avenue, Mark Cross, and I. Miller promptly moved in, much to the delight of Atlantans. Along with these legendary stalwarts, however, are a welter of smaller but equally fascinating shops—the shop of John Simmons, for instance, has really unusual gifts and lovely crystal, and Jaeger's famous woolens are there now. There are also men's and women's specialty shops in all price ranges, lovely gift and craft shops, sports boutiques, a fine book shop, two movie houses, an honest-to-goodness old-fashioned delicatessen, and a charming little restaurant on the upper level, the Peasant Uptown. Lord & Taylor's Birdcage Restaurant is good for lunch too, and there's a little soda bar in the center of the mall where you can have, if not breakfast, then at least a soda, in a curly, wrought-iron chair just outside Tiffany's. Everything is enclosed under one soaring roof, luxuriantly planted, and glittering with light from great skylights. Christmas inside the great central mall is almost as beautiful as Fifth Avenue on Christmas Eve.

You might want to combine these two shopping centers with a morning or afternoon in nearby Cates Center and Cates Plaza and Andrews Square (see "Boutique Day"), where there's unsurpassed boutiquing, but to truly savor them and save your feet we recommend you give them a day to themselves. Lenox and Phipps deserve your undivided attention. Happy hunting!

A Peachtree Shopping Tour
(*2 or more hours*)
One of Atlanta's most fascinating morning or afternoon forays is along a short stretch of Peachtree Street known to natives as Brookwood Hills. Unlike many of the newer boutique centers, it wasn't planned; like Topsy, it just grew. It's situated between the city's elegant old Brookwood Station, a midtown train station where fashionable Atlanta once entrained for their grand tours to New York and

Washington, and bustling Buckhead. It isn't a long stretch, and you finish up with lunch in one of the area restaurants that have become popular with lunchtime Atlanta.

From downtown: north on Peachtree about 3½ miles.
Park in front of stores or in lot in back.

Park your car in the big parking lot behind Clarence Foster's popular restaurant. This pretty spot, with its skylit garden court, is a great favorite with both the area's working crowd and the city's lively young crowd. If yours is an afternoon tour, you might want to start with lunch here; otherwise, keep it in mind for lunch later. Cocktails here is a fine way to finish off an afternoon tour, too. From the parking lot, walk right up Peachtree Road. The first shop you'll come to is Granny Taught Us How. Full of hand-crafted gifts and clothing, with special emphasis on beautiful quilts. Next door is the Wicker Horse, with wicker wonderments in all sizes, shapes, and price ranges. Next, you'll come to one of the city's most beloved hardware stores, Brookwood Hardware, a treasure trove of the unexpected as well as the basics. Along this stretch, too, are a small clothing shop of long standing, a flower shop whose hanging baskets and curbside wares make the sidewalk a street fair, and other interesting small nooks. Poke into each one.

Image South Gallery is one of the city's best small "serious" galleries, with regular exhibits in its front room and a fine selection of prints in back. Then there's Boots, for good examples of same; The Lemon Drop, with bright, attractive gifts and crafts; and the legendary Cloudt's Food Shop and Village Kitchen. This gourmet grocery store sells all the things you can't get anywhere else, plus delectable baked goods and take-out sandwiches, and the Cloudt brothers have catered Atlanta's most elegant parties and debuts for many years. It's a must for browsing. Next door is Skinflint's, where wines and their accouterments are inexpensive and beautifully displayed.

You'll want to go back and pick up your car now, and drive on up Peachtree, around the big curve. Next on your right is Peachtree Galleries, with *jonque extraordinaire*. Next, past a couple of restaurants, is the Onion Dome, one of the city's first emporiums of exotica. Then you'll come to Draper's Antiques, and then on to Plantasia, where the growing things are lush and vivid and varied. A bit farther on out Peachtree, you'll find shops for records, custom pillows, and more gifts and clothing. One of the city's most popular unisex hair-cutting establishments is along here, too.

The last three shops on your tour are antique shops of long standing and great favor among Atlantans. Wares at Ed Kilby's and Marsden's grace some of Atlanta's most elegant homes. And Y. Albert's has long had one of the city's most beautiful selections of oriental rugs.

If you didn't lunch at Clarence Foster's, you might want to stop at Harrison's, on your right as you drive back down Peachtree, in the center of the big curve at the light. It's one of the city's most popular oases for the with-it young, and the interiors, full of Victoriana and Art Deco appointments, are stunning. Or, you might want to drive back down Peachtree, toward downtown, and have lunch at The Coach and Six, on your right about two and a half blocks before you come to Brookwood Station. This great restaurant is one of the city's favorites for consistently fine food and service, and is a traditional mecca for Atlanta's advertising and television community. It's not strictly on your shopping tour but well worth doubling back for. And if yours was an afternoon jaunt, something cool here is a charming way to top it all off.

ANTIQUES PURE AND SIMPLE
(*4 to 8 hours*)
Every city, including Atlanta, has its quota of small, charming antique emporiums tucked away for ferreting out; so do they all have the biggies, the handful of large and spectacular shops and galleries, where it's entirely possible to spend an entire day. Atlanta has many more of the mammoths than you'll find on this tour; we've included

these because they make a logical tour and a comfortable day. This one is hard to time, because you may find yourself hopelessly enthralled in one or another and never leave; or you may want to do the lot and come back later for serious browsing at your favorite.

Start by going north on Peachtree about one mile to Elliott Antiques. Park across the street.

J. H. Elliott Antiques, at 537 Peachtree Street, really isn't all that big, but it's a must for the serious antiquer. This fine shop has been featured in *Life* magazine and is proud of its claim that many museums recommend it to discriminating buyers. English pieces are their specialty. Established in 1922, Elliott's has a national reputation for painstaking and knowledgeable appraising, as well as a simply glorious stock.

Next door is Allen, Inc., an interesting shop for home furnishings. A bit farther up Peachtree Street, at 792, is Bigg's for antiques. Almost like Rich's and Coca-Cola, Bigg's is an Atlanta institution of unquestioned lineage. The store has fine reproductions, too, but it's the antiques that draw Atlanta connoisseurs in droves.

Next, take first left off Peachtree, 2 blocks to R on Spring. Follow Spring to 1405, parking next to building.

Atlanta Galleries, at 1405 Spring Street, is mind-boggling—a glittering hodgepodge of French, English, Italian, American, and just about every other sort of antique anything you can imagine. Collections are bought and sold there regularly, and there are expert appraisers on the staff. Their sister outlet, Atlanta Auction Gallery, has regularly scheduled weekly evening auctions that are great fun even if you don't bid on anything. The Auction Gallery is at 1405 Spring Street. Call them at 876-8141 to see when the action is.

Go back to 14th Street, turn R on 14th, follow to dead end, about one mile. L Howell Mill, R one block on Brady to Turnage Place, Ltd., on left.

Turnage Place, Ltd., of Atlanta is a dignified and lovely place where the treasures are strictly bona fide, with Eng-

lish antiques a specialty. Eat your heart out . . . or bring
money.

*Then return to Howell Mill Road, L about 2 blocks
to Atlanta Antiques Exchange on right.*

Atlanta Antiques Exchange is another gigantic, eclectic
collection of English, Continental, and oriental furniture,
furnishings, and accessories; it's especially good for porcelains, crystal, and brass. The eighteenth and nineteenth
centuries predominate here, but it's possible to unearth almost anything circa anytime. If you haven't already done
it, now's the time to dig your sneakers out of your tote.

Lunch on this tour can be a bit of a problem, since it's
admittedly not close to any of Atlanta's favored spots. If
you're doing an afternoon tour, you might want to lunch
first at Salvatore's, just across from the Fox Theatre, on
upper Peachtree Street, at 669. The first two shops on the
tour are just an amble away north on Peachtree, and Salvatore's has long had some of the very best Italian cuisine
in the city—light, sophisticated, and done with a master's
touch. Park across the street in the Fox lot. Or, you'll see
several motels with restaurants at the various exits on I-75
as you return to the city.

*To return, R Howell Mill, less than 2 miles to I-75;
South for downtown, North for I-285.*

FARMERS' MARKET FORAY
(*2 or 3 hours, or all day*)
Atlanta's fabulous State Farmers' Market is to lovers of
fresh produce and growing things what Xanadu was to
Kubla Khan—a pleasure dome without peer. Gathered together here are the finest fruits of Georgia's fields, forests,
and orchards in a spectacular array of color, fragrance, and
incomparable taste. There's something going on during
each season: spring's incredible flowers and bulbs; summer's beautiful harvest of vegetables spilling over bins in
stall after stall; autumn's brilliant pumpkins and old-
fashioned ribbon cane and root vegetables. And at Christmas, acres of beautiful Christmas trees and fresh mistletoe

and exotic fruits. The Hallowe'en jack-o'-lantern and the Christmas tree from the Farmers' Market are hallowed Atlanta traditions. And, of course, there are Georgia peanuts by the bushel.

From downtown to Farmers' Market: take I-75 South. Exit Forest Parkway, L to Farmers' Market on left.

When they're in season, Georgia's fresh vegetables are something to write home about. You can also find vegetables and fruits from around the nation here, and you can take them home, too. For a late-spring-to-early-autumn tour, we suggest that you spend a morning driving up and down among the numbered sheds, choosing from the jewel-like vegetables in the individual numbered stalls. There are bargain prices for large quantities. When you've chosen your family's favorites, take them to the Farmers' Market cannery on the premises (open end of May through September). You supply the food, jars, and seals, or you may purchase cans right there, and a supervisor will help you can away to your heart's content. You can take home as many glowing jars of treasure as you can manage in a day. Even novices have no trouble and a wonderful time with the market's fine facilities and trained supervisors at their disposal. For lunch, the market cafeteria serves hearty, mouth-watering meals from fresh food brought in that day. (Breakfast is a rare treat, if you can manage to get there by the time the farmers do.) There are wonderful specialty stalls, too. Don't miss the hamper stall, where there are baskets in more sizes and shapes than you thought possible. If you're unsure what you'd like to take home with you, call 366-6910. Someone will be happy to tell you what's in season.

ET CETERA

To set out to list every shop of interest to visitors and residents in Atlanta would be to invite a small war into one's living room. The city has thousands of individual shops of interest to everyone. The ones we list here are simply some, by no means all, of *our* favorites. Most have been in business long enough to have stood the test of time; many a promising, intriguing shop has been recommended to a visitor only to have quietly closed its doors by the time he arrived on the scene. So here, in terms of durability, uniqueness, general quality, and selection of merchandise, is a handful of our favorite places to browse in Atlanta.

ROSWELL, a beautiful, ante-bellum village to our north, is pure, soothing delight. Built around a real village square, the old settlement had some of the area's stateliest ante-bellum homes, many of which are still standing and in fine repair. Along the streets bordering the square, you can see wonderful old structures such as Holly Hill, Mimosa Hall, Allenbrook, the Masonic Hall, Goulding House, Naylor Hall, the Presbyterian Church and its lovely old cemetery, Roswell Cemetery, The Bricks, Great Oaks, Barrington Hall, Minton House, and others. It's well worth your time to stroll and take in North Atlanta as it was more than a century ago. Be sure to drive west on Bulloch Street about a quarter of a mile for a look at Bulloch Hall, the white-columned, Greek Revival home of Martha (Mittie) Bulloch, mother of President Theodore Roosevelt. The President was married here in this old family home.

Also lining the square, primarily to the east, is an intriguing selection of antique and boutique purveyors. There's an exclusive women's clothing shop and intriguing emporiums for art, plants, photography, pottery, crafts, and antiques. The Roswell Historical Society is headquartered here too—drift through if you've time. The charming Public House, on the square, is fine for lunch, or you might go back for a drink or early dinner. Further on through Roswell, bearing left where the road forks, is upper Roswell, another area of antique shops and boutiques. All in all, Roswell is a mother lode of antiques and crafts.

From downtown, I-75 North, exit I-285 East (Greenville), exit Rte. 400 (Cumming), exit Northridge, turn

R, continue to Roswell Road, turn R, continue a few miles to Roswell Square.

If you have an extra hour or so, continue on for a short ramble through pretty little Crabapple.

CRABAPPLE looks as if it belongs in a tale out of Georgia's dreaming past. Little more than a country crossroads, with old Victorian brick buildings and barns standing foursquare on each corner, cows grazing in green fields, and cheerful old-timers in well-worn denim overalls, it nevertheless offers some antique and craft treasures. Try the Raven's Nest, situated in a fine, big gray barn; the Crabapple Penthouse; Morgan's Antiques; Crabapple Corners; Crabapple Emporium, for country-style foodstuffs, and accents for antiques and crafts. Browse to your heart's content; nobody's in a hurry in Crabapple.

From Roswell Square north on Rte. 19, ½ mile. L at fork marked Canton, Ga. 140. At next fork, stay straight on Crabapple Road—total 5½ miles. At blinking light is Crabapple.

DUNWOODY VILLAGE numbers among its shops some glorious pizza and ice cream, a complete range of wares for people and their homes, and one of the city's greatest grocery stores, Ogletree's. You can lounge at Sadowski's and dine at the charming J. D. Hatchery's on the beef and burgundy; and you'll want to walk around and browse. The Williamsburg motif that runs through this charming center is one of the most effective and well done we've seen.

From downtown about 15 miles: I-75 North, exit I-285 Greenville, exit Rte. 400, exit Abernathy Road-Dunwoody, straight to Chamblee-Dunwoody Road. Turn L to village.

FLEA MARKETS are so thick in Atlanta, especially in the warm months, that it's almost impossible to drive a block without running into one. The local daily newspapers and the combined Saturday and Sunday editions of the *Journal* and *Constitution* have good listings of most. Do check them if you're a flea-market buff. The largest and most established does deserve mention:

The Atlanta Flea Market, an incredible, enormous medley of people and things, holds forth each Saturday and Sunday of the month, all year; do go. While you're not apt to find any real treasure on the order of eight perfect, matching Chippendale side chairs, you're extremely apt to have the time of your life. It's the greatest show on earth.

To Atlanta Flea Market: north on Piedmont Road (3 blocks east of Peachtree) about 4 miles. Market on left.

THE BUCKHEAD BUSINESS DISTRICT, in the heart of Atlanta's creamiest residential area, is a wandering, lopsided, charming small section of unusual and eccentric shops, fine for roaming on foot or in your car, once you've turned off the tangled main artery of Peachtree Road.

Pharr Road and East Paces Ferry, in Buckhead, run parallel from Peachtree Road over to Piedmont. Take a right on either of these streets and you're in for a treat. Antiques, porcelain, crystal, leather, books, decorators' shops, plants, wine, and cheese are all housed in charming cottages that once were residences. East Paces Ferry, especially, is fine for antiquing and "jonquing." Park in the big central lot about a block down on East Paces Ferry and walk. Several little side streets connect Pharr and East Paces, and there's more intriguing browsing along each one. A favorite junket for Atlantans is a poke into the Cathedral of St. Philip's Thrift Shop on Peachtree Road, just around the corner from the public parking lot on East Paces Ferry; it's full of clothes and accessories in mint condition.

To Buckhead area from downtown: north on Peachtree about 5 miles.

THE R. L. HOPE ANTIQUE CENTER AND MAC-BRYAN ANTIQUE AUCTION was once a cherished North Atlanta grammar school and is now a fascinating labyrinth of antique shops. Each classroom is leased to an individual shopkeeper, and the school auditorium serves as an auction gallery. Auctions are held at least once a month (or by special request from groups), and you can bid on any goody you see without the usual minimum limit. Auctions are usually on weekends.

To R. L. Hope School: north on Peachtree about 5 miles to L on Piedmont; or straight north on Piedmont, cross Peachtree, and 1 block on right is schoolhouse.

WHOLESALE OUTLETS:

Wholesale outlets abound in the Atlanta area, offering bargains on everything from *haute couture* to hardware. The ones listed here are our own personal choices for good bargains in men's, women's, and children's clothing.

Loehman's, in Northeast Plaza, on the Buford Highway, has women's clothing in all sizes, much of it designer apparel. Labels have been removed, but if you know clothes, you'll recognize the quality and perhaps the designer. Sportswear, dresses, suits, coats, and furs in the winter; all yours via cash or check, all sales final. It's a regular shopping stop for chic Atlantans.

To Loehman's: I-85 North, exit Druid Hills Road-North Atlanta, R Buford Hwy. to Northeast Plaza.

The Warehouse has nationally advertised brands of junior-sized sportswear, the average reduction being about 35 per cent. Separates, pants, shirts, sweaters, and jackets are very trendy, good bargains. Cash or check, all sales final.

I-75 North, exit Howell Mill, R Chattahoochee, L Southland to L into Warehouse.

The Clothes Bin has good sportswear for the entire family, including a complete line of "active" sportswear—clothing for tennis, skiing, and the like. Good raincoats, casual coats, and sweaters for the whole family, too. Bank-Americard, C&S, and Master Charge are accepted.

To The Clothes Bin: I-75 North, exit Howell Mill, R about ½ block to store on left.

Walton Manufacturing Company, Inc., has a fine wholesale outlet for men's clothing in their factory in nearby Loganville. Suits, sports coats, and slacks hang in neat rows, with an extremely comprehensive range of styles and sizes. Alterations are done on the premises for a small charge. BankAmericard, C&S, and Master Charge are accepted.

*To Walton Manufacturing: I-85 North, exit I-285 to
Macon, exit Stone Mountain Freeway-Athens, continue
to factory on 78 when Freeway ends.*

INDIVIDUAL SHOPS:

The Wrecking Bar has a marvelous collection of antique architectural adornments, with mantels, light
fixtures, stained glass, hardware, columns, doors, entries,
shutters, and gates. Most of the wares are a bit hefty to
carry home with you, but if you're looking for a wonderful
stained-glass window, eight feet of Victorian gingerbread,
or even a gargoyle, this is the place.

*From downtown: I-20 East, exit Moreland Ave., L
Moreland just a few miles.*

The Old New York Bookshop, on Juniper Street, is a
bookworm's dream of a place to get locked into over a
long, gray winter weekend. Situated in a rambling old Victorian house, the incredible and eclectic stock of second-
hand books bulges with shelf after shelf in the high-
ceilinged old rooms. There are some real finds among
them, but it's more fun just to get reacquainted with some
old favorites. Ask for Cliff and you'll be talking books
until sometime the next day.

*From downtown: north on Piedmont, L 14th, L Ju-
niper, follow short distance to shop.*

The Atlanta Municipal Market is to Atlanta what Les
Halles once was to Paris. This incredible downtown market is a cherished Atlanta landmark and offers, under its
newly refurbished roof, row after row and stall after stall
of flowers, rare and exotic fruits and vegetables, meats,
fish, seafood, cheese, breads, complete grocery stores, snack
bars, and bakeries. It is so colorful that the Arts Festival of
Atlanta committee once threw a very posh party there,
and it's definitely the place Atlanta hostesses dash for
when they can't find fresh leeks, herbs, or whatever eso-
teric fish, fowl, or cut of meat they'd planned to serve
their guests.

*From downtown: take Courtland to L Edgewood, 2
blocks to market.*

ART IS WHERE YOU FIND IT

In Atlanta, you can find art almost anywhere you happen to be. In the traditional places, such as the High Museum of Art in the Atlanta Memorial Arts Center, with its fine permanent collection of traditional and contemporary art in all media and its wide variety of changing exhibits; in the explosion of smaller galleries all over the city (more than seventy-five at last count); in the schools, colleges, and universities that dot the city.

But with the exuberance that characterizes Atlanta, art crops up in unexpected places, too. In office buildings, restaurants, commercial lobbies, shopping malls; in parks and playgrounds; on the sides of buildings; and in open spaces between them—almost anywhere that's large enough to accommodate a piece of sculpture, a painting, or a glorious graffito. In Atlanta there is art wherever one looks—art for the connoisseur, art for kids, art for people who don't know anything about art but know what they like.

There's probably no subject quite as subjective as art. The following tours are based on simple logistics as well as merit. They're arranged so you can sample a broad selection in an easy few hours' time. The Saturday and Sunday editions of the Atlanta *Journal* and *Constitution* have pretty complete listings. The Greater Atlanta Arts Council (892-8246) can tell you what's going on in the arts in any given week.

A note: In the smaller galleries, hours fluctuate. We've listed telephone numbers for all the galleries featured in this section.

THE CONTEMPORARY CONNOISSEUR
(*About 3 hours*)
Some of the city's best contemporary art, in all media, resides in a small wedge of midtown Atlanta centering on the High Museum in the Atlanta Memorial Arts Center. The two galleries we take you to today have fine, long-

standing reputations for unearthing and showing the best and most innovative of Atlanta's contemporary artists. In addition to artists whose names are solidly established in art circles, there are regular shows by the innovative newcomers whose work will one day make important contributions to the health and vitality of art in America.

To Galerie Illien, straight on Peachtree from downtown, L 14th Street, gallery is on left.

Galerie Illien, at 124 Fourteenth Street, is one of the city's most established contemporary galleries. Special showings in addition to permanent works and a wide selection of fine contemporary art for sale. 892-2696.

To the Heath Gallery, continue on 14th Street about one block, R West Peachtree, R 15th Street, L Peachtree about half a block into Memorial Arts Center parking lot. Park in the back of the lot and walk across Lombardy Way to the Heath Gallery, in the old house directly across from the rear of the Arts Center parking lot.

The Heath Gallery, at 34 Lombardy Way, has a good selection of work in all media for sale, regularly scheduled special showings, and a fine reputation for nurturing promising newcomers. 892-2277.

To the High Museum, walk back across Lombardy, through the Arts Center parking lot, and enter the Arts Center complex at any entrance. Signs will direct you to the High Museum. Its entrance fronts on Peachtree Street.

The High Museum of Art, housed in the Atlanta Memorial Arts Center, serves the city and the Southeast as a major center for special exhibits, as well as housing a fine permanent collection. Over the years, gifts from many sources have made possible the acquisition of some extremely important collections. Keystone of the High Museum's collection is the Samuel H. Kress collection of thirty Italian Renaissance paintings. The Uhry print collection is also outstanding. The contemporary collection is fascinating and is constantly being expanded under the di-

rection of the museum's dynamic young director, Gud-
mund Vigtel. Special exhibits of outstanding quality are
scheduled throughout the year, and a special Junior Gallery offers innovative art for the small fry to see, touch,
and experience. There are fine prints and other objects for
sale in the museum's excellent shop. Be sure to see
Auguste Rodin's magnificent mourning figure in bronze,
L'Ombre (The Shade), given to the city in 1968 by the
Republic of France as a tribute to 122 Atlanta art patrons
who died in an air crash in Paris in 1962 while on a cultural tour of Europe.

If you're in the area at lunchtime, walk across Peachtree
Street from the Museum to Colony Square and have a
bite at Brothers Two. It's dark and attractive, the lunch
menu is ample, and you'll rub elbows with representatives
of Atlanta's flourishing advertising community. While
you're in Colony Square, you might want to browse
through the Galleria Markus of Venezia, also in the complex, or drop in at the offices of the Arts Council of
Greater Atlanta to see what's up elsewhere in Atlanta's art
world that week.

If you'd like to take this tour without your car, catch
any one of the downtown buses marked Peachtree and
ride as far as 14th Street. Get off at 14th Street and
walk down to the Galerie Illien, back up to Peachtree
and 1 block north to visit the High Museum, across the
rear parking lot of the museum to Lombardy and the
Heath Gallery, then back up to Peachtree and catch a
bus back downtown. It's a pleasant ride, an easy stroll,
and costs very little indeed.

BUCKHEAD BEAUX ARTS
(5 to 6 hours)
Buckhead is the ground-zero center of Atlanta's affluent
northside, and also the home of some of the city's most
avant-garde small galleries and shops. This tour will take
you to two of the city's most contemporary galleries, a
one-of-a-kind arts and crafts shop, and a sculpture garden

that has to be experienced to be believed. We'd suggest that you see the first in the morning, have lunch in the area, and devote the afternoon to the garden. Or reverse the order, if you like. Either way, give this tour most of a day.

One of the city's newer galleries, Image South, at 1931 Peachtree Road, has regularly scheduled special exhibits of fine contemporary work in all media and a good selection of prints and paintings for sale. 351-3179.

To Image South: north on Peachtree just a few miles.

The Signature Shop, at 3767 Roswell Road, has signed, one-of-a-kind original American crafts and really lovely paintings, pottery, sculpture, wall hangings, weaving, and other art objects. It's an Atlanta landmark. If Blanche Reeves is around, ask her to tell you about the origin of some of your favorites. Regular hours six days a week, since it's a shop.

To Signature Shop: continue north on Peachtree about 2 miles, L at fork to Roswell; just a few blocks on right in small shopping area is the shop.

Barclay Galleries, in Phipps Plaza, at 3500 Peachtree Road, features signed, limited-edition original graphics from modern American and European artists. Very sleek and contemporary. 233-8712.

While you're in Phipps, walk around the upper gallery from the Barclay Galleries to the Peasant Uptown, directly across, and have lunch. This courtyard-greenhouse restaurant has wonderful plants and a good luncheon menu, including a hearty and savory *quiche* that makes all others pale by comparison. Lunch on the gallery outside, if you can, and watch the crowds at play below. There's also a pretty little soda-and-sandwich shop on the lower mall at Phipps Plaza, just outside Tiffany's, where you can relax and crowd-watch in old-fashioned ice cream chairs. Also, an uncommonly good delicatessen makes its home just down the passageway from the mall-level soda shop.

To Barclay: continue north on Roswell Road, R Hab-ersham (runs into Piedmont), continue R on Pied-

mont, L Peachtree. A few blocks on left is Phipps Plaza.

In the heart of Atlanta's shady northwest section is the home of Carley Craig, one of the city's most beloved and versatile artists. This extraordinary woman has turned her natural, tree-vaulted garden into a sculpture garden of supreme strength, tranquillity, and serenity. Soaring metal and stone abstractions placed at strategic points along the paths that bisect the garden make for a quiet half hour or so of reflection and inspiration. Nothing makes Miss Craig happier than the knowledge that her work gives back to its viewers some of the joy and vibrancy that inspired her to create it. Her studio is here too, but she is a working artist, and while visitors are welcome to her garden when she can accommodate them, she asks that they call ahead before coming. Her number is 355-6058. A gentle and extremely talented woman, Carley Craig has in her garden and heart an abundance of the riches of the human spirit.

If you wish to start this tour at Carley Craig's sculpture garden, take I-75 from downtown to Northside exit (first exit after 14th Street). Miss Craig will give you the street address and exact instructions when you call. From her garden, continue north on Northside Drive, R Collier Road, L Peachtree about half a block to Image South Gallery. Follow regular tour directions from there.

CITYSCAPE
(2 to 5 hours)

Downtown Atlanta is a work of art in progress. In no other area of the city does art come so vibrantly, robustly alive; in sculpture, in informal graffiti, in vivid supergraphics on exterior walls, in lobbies and halls and shops and urban complexes. In other areas, art resides in small, cloistered galleries which are perfect for leisurely contemplation and quiet perusal. Downtown, you get out and mingle with the people. And the result is art as, perhaps, it was really meant to be—a brawling, breathing, joyous part of everyday life. This tour, we think, combines the very best of the arts downtown.

A note: You might want to leave your car at Peachtree Center and walk part of the tour; it *can* be done, though it makes for a strenuous day. But it's the best way we know to see the burgeoning supergraphics on city walls and the pockets of sculpture springing up downtown. In that case, have lunch downtown and see the museum afterward. Or, if you're short on time, drive it.

From northern Atlanta: South I-75 or I-85, exit Williams, L Harris; park in any one of numerous lots. Peachtree and Harris—2 blocks from Williams—is beginning of Peachtree Center. From southern Atlanta: North on I-75/I-85, exit International Blvd.; park in garage on International just past Ivy. You are across from Peachtree Center.

Peachtree Center, Atlanta's soaring urban complex designed by world-famous architect John Portman, is a giant art gallery in itself. Within this complex of hotels, offices, shopping malls, restaurants, cafés, and theatres, there's sculpture at every turn. And within Peachtree Center there are three good galleries that you'll want to see. The Signature Shop features exquisite, signed, one-of-a-kind wall hangings, weavings, paintings, pottery, and other *objets d'art* from American artists and craftsmen. The Mint Gallery, in the Cain Tower, has an excellent selection of traditional and contemporary art in all media. The small Regency Gallery, in the Hyatt Regency Hotel, is elegant and inviting. All have wares for sale, but you may just browse. Anne Jacobs' first-rate contemporary gallery is in Peachtree Center too, as is Hans Frabel's legendary crystal.

Drive south on Peachtree about 1 mile, L Wall Street, L into parking garage. You will walk back 2 short blocks to begin this tour at Trust Company of Georgia.

One of the most exciting new art happenings downtown is found in the lobby of the Trust Company of Georgia

Building. The art and sculpture you'll see here is a co-operative venture between the trust company, the High Museum of Art, the Art Department of Georgia State University, and Central Atlanta Progress. This fine, eclectic, continuing exhibit features works selected by the High Museum, drawn from many sources, and is an ongoing, ever-changing joy for visitors and regular downtowners alike.

From trust company, we suggest you walk to Underground Atlanta.

In Underground Atlanta, our fabled "City Beneath a City" that is a loving re-creation of the city as it was in the lusty ante-bellum days of the railroads, you'll find the Golden Easel Gallery. This is a serious gallery, despite its gala, just-for-fun environs; some of the region's most notable artists show here regularly, and there's a good selection of art for sale. By all means, poke around Underground, but save the serious exploring in Underground for another day. There's more art coming.

From garage, R Wall, R Peachtree, L Marietta, cross Techwood to Omni parking on right.

The fabulous Omni International Atlanta is another of the city's gleaming, futuristic urban complexes; it's so spectacular that you'll be tempted to dawdle through the entire edifice. In the midst of the luxury shopping, the movie theatres and restaurants, and the ice-skating rink, you'll find the exceptionally fine Arnold Gallery, with some of the Southeast's most innovative contemporary work. Give it plenty of time, because it's well up to Omni standards.

If you're hungry, the Omni is the place for lunch. There are several restaurants under its roof, offering various international cuisines, all good. Browse around and name your manna.

Throughout the downtown area, we hope you'll take special notice of the glorious, monumental painted exterior walls that add so much joy and color to Atlanta's downtown ambience. They're called urban walls and are a joint project of the Arts Festival of Atlanta and Central Atlanta Progress. At present, there are six, with more coming. If you'd like a map showing their locations, so you can walk the routes, call Central Atlanta Progress, at 658-1877.

RESTORATION ATLANTA

Atlanta has always been a city of neighborhoods. Compared to some of the great cities of the South, such as Charleston, New Orleans, and Savannah, we're a relatively young city, and more than one of our sister cities have always considered us a rawboned country upstart of a town. But our graceful old Victorian neighborhoods evoke a gentle, leisurely past of their own. They've lived through periods of great growth and progress and periods of hard luck and tight money, through world wars and social change, and the last great spurt of growth that brought Atlanta to world eminence. Over the years, many of the once-proud old communities slipped gently into decay, dreaming of their golden past, while the present roared around them and the future took shape on their doorsteps. But most are back and booming now, and well worth a long look.

This tour takes you to four of the city's most spectacular areas of restoration: the West End, Inman Park, Midtown, and Ansley Park. Some, like Ansley Park, are now the most select neighborhoods to live in the entire city; others, like the West End, are still in the process of getting there. See it all; it's Atlanta as it was, is, and will be.

VIGOR, VISION, AND VICTORIANA
(4 to 4½ hours with lunch, 3 hours without lunch)
The first neighborhood on your tour will be the West End, a fine old neighborhood of ante-bellum-to-Victorian houses that grew up around the White Hall Tavern, a stagecoach stop built in the early 1830s, before Terminus (later named Atlanta) existed. By the beginning of the Civil War, there were a number of lovely homes here, many belonging to the most prominent Atlantans of the day; and when the city was rebuilt after the war, the most imposing houses were built here. By 1880, West End was home to a large section of elegant Atlanta. Former Secre-

tary of State Dean Rusk grew up in this section of
Atlanta.

In 1957, talk of restoration began to stir in the sadly
shabby but still lovely old section, and local and federal
government ultimately joined forces to rehabilitate many
of the public areas and facilities there. Since 1966 alone,
more than 1,100 structures have been restored, and several
new parks are coming. The most visible—and heart-warm-
ing—efforts, however, have been devoted to the old Victorian houses, a movement spearheaded by young Atlanta
architect Wade Burns. He moved into one of the old
houses and, since, has purchased more than twenty in a
two-block area. Great co-operation from the Department
of Housing and Urban Development has made it possible
for the buyers of these houses to assume extremely low-in-
terest loans when they move in, and today the area is
fondly called "Atlanta's Georgetown." As you drive, you'll
see incredible gingerbread sparkling on the turreted old
houses, smart new brickwork, gas lamps, and pristine
lawns. To leave the shadows of soaring, futuristic Peachtree Center and drive back through Atlanta's past is a fascinating foray into history.

Peeples Street is the heart of the West End restoration
area; notice, as you drive, the brick sidewalks and arches,
gas lamps, sparkling houses, and neighborhood businesses.
A walking tour of the West End will enchant you; if
you'd like to do it, the area of Peeples Street is the place
to start.

   *From downtown, enter I-75/I-85 South, bear right to
   I-20W, exit Ashby (third exit after I-85), L Ashby, 3
   blocks to R Oglethorpe, R Peeples Street.*

The rambling old Victorian Wren's Nest is the ances-
tral home of Atlanta's beloved Joel Chandler Harris,
whose vivid imagination and fluent pen gave birth to the
wonderful Uncle Remus stories. Here you'll see the original mailbox where, on a fine summer day, a wren built her
nest and raised her family undisturbed, and so named the
house. Much Harris memorabilia is still in the old home:

Harris' desk, countless photos, and his treasury of books. On the grounds, you can still see "Thimblefinger Well," "Snap Bean Farm," and the infamous "Briar Patch," just as Harris wrote about them in *Uncle Remus*.

From Peeples Street, L on MLK Blvd., you'll come to the Wren's Nest ½ block on the left.

Five Points is the heart of the "old" Atlanta business district, as well as the new, named for five rambling, bustling downtown streets that come together there. It is the heart of Atlanta's financial district, and the towering skyscrapers you see are almost bound to be banks, savings and loan institutions, or other financial institutions. As you drive down Marietta Street through Five Points, turn L on Peachtree and drive down Edgewood Avenue. On your left is Central City Park. Hardly a day passes in spring and summer when something fun isn't going on in the park. You'll soon see the triangular Hurt Building at Edgewood and Exchange Place, built in 1913 by pioneer skyscraper builder Joel C. Hurt. Beyond the building is Hurt Park, which is spectacular in the spring with thousands of tulips and flowering bulbs. A bit farther down, at the corner of Edgewood and Courtland, you'll see the funny little Victorian building that housed the original Coca-Cola Bottling Company. It's now the Baptist Student Union Center for Georgia State University.

From the Wren's Nest, R MLK Blvd., L Peeples, R Oak Street, L Ashby, R I-20 East, exit Windsor-Spring, go about 1 mile, R Marietta Street through Five Points.

Inman Park owes its existence to the above-mentioned Joel Hurt and his conception of an electric streetcar line linking a garden suburb and a large office building. The streetcar line, Atlanta's first, opened in 1899, and by that time, Inman Park, developed as an English garden city suburb, was well underway. When the automobile came chugging into Atlanta, many residents moved to the country—present midtown Atlanta—and Inman Park's glorious old houses and tree-shaded streets became unfashionable and sunk out of sight. By 1960, ringed with industrial sprawl, the park was a slum. But it was, and is today, the city's only area of late-nineteenth- and early-twentieth-century houses; and as Atlanta's commuting problems began to become really severe, Inman Park began to look feasible once more as a good place to live. In 1969, young Atlanta designer Robert Griggs bought the park's most important house, a wonderful old sprawl of a structure at 866 Euclid Avenue, and restored it with love and taste, thereby setting off a renaissance in Inman. Many other old houses have been restored by other young Atlantans, and the park is now local legend. Inman Park has, as do most of the other restored areas of the city, countless small flea markets and fairs, as well as a large annual spring tour of houses. A flip through the Atlanta newspapers in the spring can tell you when. Drive it and enjoy; Inman Park is a renaissance of the human spirit as well as a neighborhood.

L Peachtree at the First National Bank Building; Peachtree runs into Edgewood if you continue straight; out Edgewood about 2 miles. When approaching the fork of Edgewood and Euclid, get in right lane. Continue on Edgewood, L Waverly Way, R Euclid, L Elizabeth, L Waverly, R Euclid, R Druid Circle, R Euclid . . . 1 block, R Spruce, L Dixie, L Waddell, R Edgewood, R Piedmont.

You'll be lunching today at one of the most spectacular Victorian houses in Atlanta and the South, and perhaps the country: the Mansion. The Mansion Restaurant occupies a part of the old Edward C. Peters house on a full city block at the corner of Piedmont and Ponce de Leon Avenue. Ivy Hall, as it was named when it was built, in 1885, is a grand Victorian fantasy of turrets, arches, spires, gingerbread, and other fanciful oddments, and is a fitting monument to the man whose dealings in real estate virtually changed the face of the city. Members of the Peters family lived there until 1970, and the addition of the restaurant has not changed the house's charming ambience.

At Ivy Hall, no two rooms are alike, and the ivy motif is carried out in carvings throughout the house. You'll enjoy looking as much as lunching at the Mansion. (If you've time on your way to lunch, you might take a short detour and drive by the famed Ebenezer Baptist Church, where Atlanta's beloved Dr. Martin Luther King, Jr., shared the pulpit with his father, our beloved "Daddy King," the adjacent King gravesite with its eternal flame, and Dr. King, Jr.'s birthplace.)

From Piedmont, R Auburn, L Boulevard, L Irwin, R Piedmont. Go about a mile and cross North Avenue; Mansion on right.

After lunch, get ready to tour a small but fascinating in-city neighborhood known simply as Midtown. This area grew up in the early 1900s, as people began to move out into the rural countryside from what is downtown Atlanta today. In a transitional state of development until recently, the area was inhabited by older residents who had always lived there and younger business and professional people who liked the convenience to downtown, the tree-lined sidewalks, the small lawns, and the individually styled houses; they are rare attributes in an area so close to the heart of the city. In 1969, several area churches rallied neighborhood residents to become acquainted with one another, and the resulting coalition led to the formation of the Midtown Association. With the aid of some of the city's most imaginative young architects and designers, who now live there, Midtown has begun to bloom again, as you'll see when you drive past the architecturally innovative restorations, the newly planted trees and shrubs, and the spanking-new paint and manicured lawns. There are two houses of particular note. One is at 821 Piedmont Avenue, at the corner of Sixth Street. Completed in 1892, it is a fine example of Victoriana, right down to the silver-plated interior hardware. The house has been nominated for inclusion on the National Register.

The house at 835 Myrtle Street, now owned by a local bank executive, was once the home of Ralph McGill, well-known former editor and publisher of the Atlanta *Constitution*.

> *From Piedmont, R 8th Street, R Durant Place, R 6th Street, R Argonne, L 6th Street, R Myrtle Street, L 10th Street, R Piedmont.*

You're now on the fringes of one of Atlanta's most fascinating and desirable in-town neighborhoods, Ansley Park. To your right and stretching away for miles is the city's beloved Piedmont Park, which Atlantans use rather like a large outdoor living room all year. It was the scene of the fabled Cotton States Exposition in 1895 (prompting John Philip Sousa to compose his "King Cotton March"). The city's magnificent greenhouses are here, as are a lovely *bonsai* garden, a lake and duck ponds, baseball diamonds, and a good golf course; swings for lovers and lunchers; and all kinds of people doing all kinds of wonderful, wacky things all year long. The park's annual spring Arts Festival of Atlanta is a solid week of art, sculpture, dance, drama, music, and crafts, but it's fun anytime.

> *From Piedmont, L 14th Street, R Peachtree, R 15th, L Peachtree Circle, R Westminster, R Prado, immediate R Barksdale, R Lafayette, L Yonah, L 15th, R Piedmont to downtown Atlanta.*

A note: The apartment building at South Prado, at the corner of Piedmont, was the home of Atlanta's legendary Margaret Mitchell and her husband, John Marsh, at the time of her death. And the soaring complex of office towers and condominiums that lean over the green island of Ansley Park is Colony Square, one of Atlanta's proudest and most innovative in-town commercial-residential complexes. Here is the magnificent Fairmont Hotel, with its elegant restaurants, lounges, and nightclubs; a mammoth ice-skating rink, some of the city's smartest shops and boutiques; and a welter of Atlanta's most high-powered advertising agencies. If you're a bit wilted, why not stop off for a quiet drink in one of the Fairmont's many bistros or the excellent Brothers Two Restaurant, stroll around a bit, and just enjoy?

THAT'S RIGHT ... WALK!

Atlantans walk in droves, as any spring noon hour or crystal fall day downtown will prove. Indeed, given the city's charming but decidedly offhand tangle of downtown streets, it's by far the easiest way to get around. And there's a wealth to see in our downtown district; not only the polished, monumental mini-city complexes that are recarving our skyline, but the amusing little inklings and oddments of shops and services that still survive amid the monoliths, like defiant daffodils in a redwood forest. In fact, to really savor Atlanta's heart, you *must* walk it; you'll be amply rewarded. Watch for the monumental, colorful urban wall paintings you'll see scattered around; a joint project of Central Atlanta Progress and the Arts Festival of Atlanta, they bring great joy to our downtown area.

The tours in this section will concentrate on two areas of Atlanta's downtown that are especially pleasant and interesting to walk. You may find other intriguing strolls, but for a newcomer or a suburbanite seeking to get reacquainted with the central city, these two cover the waterfront, as it were.

CAPITOL CAPER
(*About 3 hours or more, depending on stops for exhibits, tours, and lunch*)
This tour will take you through Atlanta's unique Tri-Governmental complex, one of very few such areas in the nation, and to Underground Atlanta, a fascinating re-creation of an entire area of Atlanta that sprang up around the brawling, bustling railroad yards in the early and middle years of the nineteenth century.

You'll start your tour by parking in the lot on MLK Blvd., at Underground Atlanta. If you're coming downtown from the expressway, exit MLK Blvd., bear R two blocks and park. Walk back up MLK Blvd. two blocks

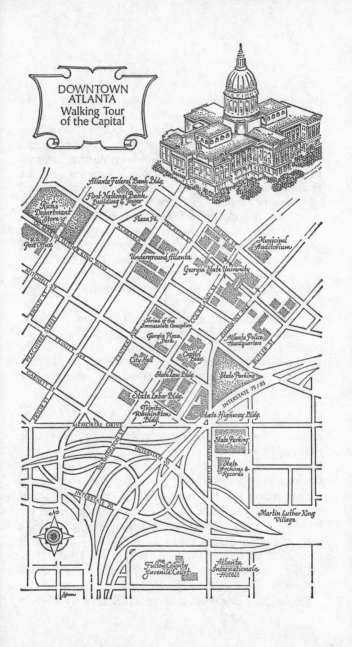

DOWNTOWN ATLANTA
Walking Tour of the Capital

Atlanta Federal Bank Bldg.

First National Bank Building & Tower

Rich's Department Store

U.S. Post Office

Plaza Pk.

Underground Atlanta

Municipal Auditorium

Georgia State University

Shrine of the Immaculate Conception

Georgia Plaza Park

City Hall

Capitol Bldg.

Atlanta Police Headquarters

State Law Bldg.

State Parking

State Labor Bldg.

Trinity Washington Bldg.

State Highway Bldg.

MEMORIAL DRIVE

INTERSTATE 75 / 85

INTERSTATE 20

State Parking

State Archives & Records

INTERSTATE 20

Martin Luther King Village

Fulton County Juvenile Court

Atlanta Internationale Hotel

MITCHELL

BROAD ST.

PEACHTREE

TRINITY AVE.

GARNETT ST.

PRYOR ST.

WASHINGTON ST.

CAPITOL AVENUE

COURT LAND ST.

PIEDMONT AVE.

BUTLER ST.

CENTRAL

MARTIN LUTHER KING BLVD.

ALABAMA

DECATUR

CAPITOL AVE.

to Capitol Avenue, three blocks on Capitol Avenue to Georgia Department of Archives Building. Or take a cab to the Archives Building and begin your tour. If time is short and you don't plan to tour it, you may want to view it from MLK Blvd.

The Georgia Department of Archives is one of the most fascinating spots in the city for browsing. The receptionist just inside the door will give you directions for a self-guided tour; be sure to see the displays and artifacts in the vestibule and the stunning stained-glass panorama entitled "The Rise and Fall of the Confederacy," just to the right of the lovely old Honduran-mahogany staircase as you ascend. The rare-manuscripts room is unique, a treasure trove of documents and articles that are priceless links from Atlanta's then to our now. The Archives Building has what is considered to be one of the most advanced systems in the world for the preservation of old documents. Special tours highlighting this delicate science may be arranged.

Retrace your route back to MLK Blvd. and visit the Georgia State Capitol Building.

The Georgia State Capitol is the nucleus of Atlanta's Tri-Governmental complex, which includes state, county and city governmental offices. The Georgia statehouse is built of Indiana limestone and gilded with real gold, brought from Dahlonega in North Georgia, where one of America's very first gold rushes took place. Inside, a series of busts commemorate Georgia's most famous native sons, and the fourth-floor museum of state resources, products, and events is interesting and informative. Guided building tours are fun and free if you've time; ask at the information desk in the lobby and on the second floor. Also, the Georgia General Assembly convenes in January and February, and it's often possible to get passes to the House at the speaker's office and to the Senate at the lieutenant governor's office.

From the Capitol, stroll across Washington Street to Georgia Plaza Park.

Georgia Plaza Park is a wonderful way station for a walk, and a joy to behold in itself. In practically every season of the year, it's a multi-level garden spot with glorious plantings. Fall chrysanthemums and spring bulbs are pleasing to the eye, and comfortable benches for resting and crowd-watching are plentiful. In all weather, a charming garden room dispenses quick foods and salads—a good idea if you're in the mood for lunch or refreshments. Or, if you started after lunch, hold off until Underground and have an early dinner.

Cross Mitchell Street from Plaza Park to City Hall. Atlanta's City Hall, built in 1930, is known locally (and fondly) as "The Painted Lady of Mitchell Street," largely because of its ornate, Art Deco lobby. Built by Ten Eyck Brown, it's a unique mini-skyscraper, with luxurious lobby detailing in the classic travertine, marble, and bronze of the 30s. The interior has been compared to the interior of the Fox Theatre.

From City Hall, turn L to Central Avenue and R on Central. If you walk one block along Central Avenue, you'll see the buildings devoted to Fulton County government. Like many of the structures in the Tri-Governmental complex, except the State Capitol, they're erected of marble quarried in North Georgia's famous marble pits. On the corner of Central Avenue and MLK Boulevard stands the Church of the Immaculate Conception, a well-loved Atlanta landmark. The original Catholic church that stood on this spot was in the path of General Sherman, who was in a hurry to get out of town, and the church's first pastor, Father O'Reilly, is credited with persuading the General to spare Immaculate Conception and Atlanta's other churches. There's a plaque honoring Father O'Reilly on the grounds of City Hall.

Just across from Immaculate Conception is the entrance to Underground Atlanta, an absolute must even if your feet are killing you. Stop off for a cool drink in one of its

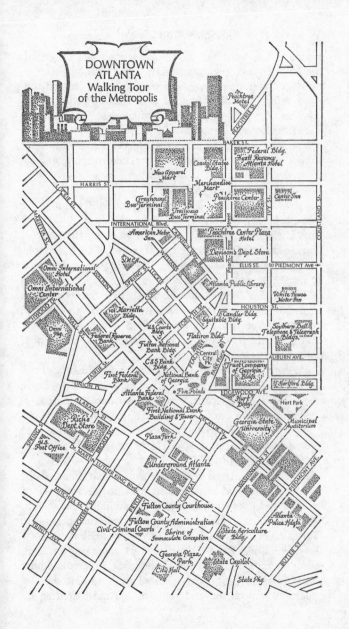

bistros if you need a rest. This charming "City Beneath the City" is an authentic restoration of the shops, saloons, cafés, cobblestones, banks, and warehouses of our fast-and-loose young railroad days, and a wonderful welter of restaurants, nightclubs, shops, exhibits, museums, and special attractions have been added. See it all, and when you're done, your car will be in the parking lot, waiting for you; or there's always a cab back to where you're going.

DOWNTOWN FOOTNOTES

(*2 hours at a leisurely pace; or many more if you stop for tours, exhibits, and lunch*)

This is the best route we know for covering the most of downtown Atlanta in one pleasant, comprehensive ramble. This can be quite a long tour, depending on the number of stops you make, so pick yourself a good day or pack a folding umbrella in your tote and bring out your most trusted old walking shoes. This isn't the day to break in new ones. We wouldn't advise it on a very hot or very cold day either; fortunately, the city has relatively few of both.

Begin your tour by parking in the Continental Trailways Bus Terminal: I-85 South, exit Williams, L Harris, R Spring; I-85 North, exit International, 4 blocks, R Spring, L into parking; and walk through the connecting covered walkway to Peachtree Center. Or take a cab or a bus to Peachtree and Harris streets, where Peachtree Center is situated.

Peachtree Center is the urban center that changed the face of Atlanta and attracted the eyes of the world. Here, in this series of interconnecting buildings and plazas, architect John Portman has assembled the innovative Hyatt Regency Atlanta Hotel and the soaring, seventy-story Peachtree Plaza Hotel, a great merchandise mart, offices, restaurants, a beautiful shopping gallery, a dinner theatre without peer, lushly planted malls and arcades and pedestrian concourses, and some of the most exciting indoor-outdoor sculpture in the world. Stroll around; there are plenty of places to linger and rest awhile.

From Peachtree Center, walk south one block to Ellis, R to Carnegie, L to the Atlanta Public Library.

The lovely old Carnegie Library, housing Atlanta's central public library facility, was built in 1910 and is now woefully inadequate for the library's vast stock of books and other materials. A recent bond referendum has provided funds for a new central library, designed by internationally known architect Marcel Breuer, so the fate of the old building is still unknown. But it's a lovely and peaceful spot to rest and read and browse, and there's a good small memorial library with the effects of Margaret Mitchell, who, ironically, wanted no memorial at all. After she wrote *Gone with the Wind*, Miss Mitchell asked that many of her effects be destroyed after her death, but some remain, and they make for fascinating browsing.

From the Carnegie Library, cross the street and turn right to Peachtree Street.

The theatre staring you in the face is Loew's Grand, scene of the world premiere of *Gone with the Wind*. It started life in 1893 as the De Give Opera House and was converted into an Art Deco movie palace in 1932. Though it's not so spruce now, and the theatre shares the building with a hodgepodge of offices and novelty shops, the interior still remains as it was on the great occasion of the premiere of the extraordinary movie.

The triangular building just down the way and across from Loew's Grand is the city's oldest surviving skyscraper. Built in 1897, the building's original occupant was the Georgia Savings Bank. The Hamilton Bank, now out of business, recently completed a massive restoration of the building, and it's truly lovely; do peek into the lobby and see how high finance looked in the gay nineties.

A bit farther down on Peachtree, at 127, is the Candler Building, built in 1906 by Asa G. Candler, who made Coca-Cola a household word. It was by far the most lavish of the early skyscrapers and caused a great furor on opening day. This building, too, has undergone recent and extensive restoration, and its incredible lobby is a wonder of marble, gilt, and bronze, with virtually every level square inch carved and curled.

Continue on Peachtree 2 blocks to Central City Park.

Central City Park, in front of the Trust Company of Georgia Building, often has something gay and slightly wacky going on. Here you can savor sunshine and planting along with street bands, dance exhibits, hula-hoop and Frisbee contests, an executive hopscotch session—almost anything you can imagine. Rest a while and enjoy. Then wander into the lobby of the Trust Company building, where one of the city's most exciting art happenings is to be found. This fine, eclectic, continuing exhibit of art and sculpture is a co-operative venture between the Trust Company, the High Museum of Art, the Art Department of Georgia State University, and Central Atlanta Progress. Works are drawn from many sources and selected by the High Museum. It's a joy.

Continue to First National Bank Tower at Peachtree and Marietta streets, walk west on Marietta 2 blocks to Henry Grady statue.

You're now in the very heart of Atlanta's financial district, where almost any tall building you happen to see is a bank or a savings-and-loan institution. The statue on the island in mid-intersection is of Henry Grady, one of the city's great statesmen and newspaper editors, who, after the Civil War, coined a phrase Atlanta still claims: "A city too busy to hate." At the corner of Marietta and Forsyth streets is the First Federal Savings and Loan Building, where an exact duplicate of the law office used by President Woodrow Wilson in 1883, while he was a young Atlanta lawyer, can be found. It is open to the public.

Continuing on Marietta, you'll notice on your left the imposing Federal Reserve Bank and the new Atlanta Newspapers, Inc., building, both fine places to visit if you've time. Tours are by appointment, so call ahead if you'd like to take one.

Two of Atlanta's most noteworthy institutions lie ahead of you now, one a cherished old shopping tradition and one a sparkling new one. To sample the old, turn left at Marietta and Spring streets and stroll a short distance down Spring to Rich's Department Store. Enter by Store for Homes. The love affair between Atlanta and Rich's is legendary. If a store can be said to embody the spirit of a city, Rich's does so for Atlanta. Rich's is far more than just a fashion trend setter, though it's that, too; you can buy literally anything, arrange a tour, or get your car serviced. It's been an integral part of the city for more than a century.

For the new but no less fabled, continue straight on Marietta Street at the Spring Street intersection and you'll come to the space-age world of Omni International Atlanta. Here is a futuristic sports arena that is home to the Atlanta Flames hockey team and the Atlanta Hawks basketball team; a luxurious, 500-room hotel; an international shopping bazaar and luxury shopping island, where such names as Lanvin, Pucci, and Hermes spread their goods; and an enormous ice-skating rink. Here, too, are several fine restaurants, offering every variety of cuisine imaginable; six movie houses; an indoor meditation garden designed by Atlanta's well-known landscape architect Jim Kluttz; offices; and some of the South's great entertainment in the form of concerts, circus performances, and ice shows. Unbelievable, and definitely a good place to stop for a rest, drink, a bite, and a browse. Then you can just go back down Marietta to Spring, walk northeast about four blocks to the Trailways Terminal and your car; or catch a convenient cab at the Omni—and so, perhaps, to bed.

DAYTIME AND THEN SOME

As we said before, you probably couldn't use up daytime Atlanta during the space of one lifetime if you tried. These daytime tours cover a lot, but there's even more, a host of under-the-sun things to do that don't fall naturally into an organized tour but are not to be missed, either. Besides the large, spectacular attractions you can attend any time of the year, such as Stone Mountain Park, Kingdoms 3, Underground Atlanta (glorious Six Flags over Georgia is closed during the winter months), and the galleries and museums, there are smaller—but no less fun—things popping all over in daytime Atlanta, on a seasonal or year-round basis, that we think you might like to sample, and some wonderful spots to visit. Be sure to check the Saturday and Sunday editions of the Atlanta newspapers for a treasure trove of them. Study them before you set out anywhere.

The Atlanta Symphony Orchestra has Sunday afternoon concerts during its regular fall-winter season, and a marvelous series of summer pops concerts at the pavilion at Stone Mountain Park on Sunday afternoons. Pack a lunch and go. Or on Friday evenings to Chastain Park. Both are hands-down Atlanta favorites. Call 892-3600 for pops information and tickets, or pick them up at the gate. Regular symphony tickets and information, 892-3600.

The Atlanta Public Library, downtown at 126 Carnegie Way, has a wonderful series of daily activities at lunchtime, ranging from yoga and exercises to daily films to puppet shows to slide presentations to just about anything else, plus special scheduled activities. Call 522-9363 to see what's happening when, or drop by and pick up a monthly activities sheet. (Card holders can call and have them sent.) Branch libraries all over town have special attractions during daylight hours, too.

Dinner-theatre matinees are a fine way to spend an afternoon. The spectacular Midnight Sun Dinner Theatre, in Peachtree Center, has them on Wednesdays and Sundays, and throws in a charming fashion show along with an opulent meal and a fine production. Reservations, 577-7074. And Atlanta's perennial favorites, the Wits End Players, present their fine madness on Tuesdays at lunchtime at the Sheraton-Biltmore Hotel, on West Peachtree Street. Reservations: 881-9500. The charming Harlequin Dinner Theatre has Wednesday matinees too. Reservations: 262-1552.

Regular theatres offer matinee fare, too; both the excellent Theatre of the Stars Winter Play Season, at the Peachtree Playhouse, 892-4110, and the Alliance Theatre, in the Memorial Arts Center, 892-2797, offer Sunday matinee performances in season.

Travelogs are immensely popular with Atlantans, and there's a fine Sunday afternoon series in Symphony Hall during the fall and winter season. Phone 892-2414 to find out about them.

The Walter Hill Auditorium, in the Memorial Arts Center, has been Sunday afternoon headquarters for Atlantans for many years, especially in the fall and winter months. Lectures, slide presentations, seminars, forums on everything under the sun, plus films and special events. Call 892-2414 to see what's doing.

McElreath Hall, on the grounds of the Atlanta Historical Society, on West Andrews Drive, just off West Paces Ferry Road to the left, has a continuing program of special multi-media exhibits and presentations based on Atlanta's past, present, and future—spectacularly done and most impressive. Catch the show daily and on Saturday; they run continuously during operating hours. Swan House, the Swan Coach House and Restaurant, and the Tullie Smith House, here, are fine to explore daily too.

The Coca-Cola Company, 310 North Avenue, N.W., has a spectacular visitor center and a wonderful collection of Coca-Cola memorabilia. Browse through an enchanting exhibit of Coca-Cola arts and artifacts from the days when it was a modest little headache remedy up to now. Open

to groups by appointment Monday through Friday from
10:00 A.M. to 3:00 P.M. Call 897-2121 for more information.

The Fulton Federal Savings & Loan Gem Collection, at
3451 Peachtree Road, N.E., across from Phipps Plaza, has
a magnificent collection of gems from around the world.
Cut and uncut, used in artifacts or displayed alone, these
beautiful gems and other minerals dazzle the eye and lift
the heart, and they're on display for free. Call 586-7404
for more information.

Oakland Cemetery, in the Southeast section of the city
near downtown, is Atlanta's oldest cemetery, and the final
resting place of many Confederate heroes, city pioneers,
and civic movers and shakers. The whole history of the
city is written here, on curly old marble and granite monu-
ments, and it's a lovely, peaceful place to wander. Many
Atlantans picnic here, with due respect, of course, and our
beloved Margaret Mitchell sleeps here, too. You can visit
during daylight hours any day, but it's off limits on Hallowe'en. Call 688-0733 for more information.

Atlanta colleges and universities have outstanding concert, lecture, dance, and art series during the fall and winter, not to mention first-rate dramatic presentations. Many
of these, especially the concert and lecture series, have
Sunday afternoon performances. The weekend editions of
the Atlanta papers have a complete list of college cultural
fare.

Note: "In season," where you see it in reference to
theatres and other cultural events, means late fall through
early spring.

Nighttime Atlanta

Atlanta by night is an artist's study in motion, fluidity, color, sound, taste, ambience. It can be velvety and caressing, low-key and intimate, brassy and big-time, raucous and often raunchy, elegant to the point of caricature, inelegant to the limit of the law. It can start as early as 4:00 P.M. happy hour and last until breakfast. It can be costlier than a weekend at the Green Door or as inexpensive as a free concert in the park. It can mean chamber music in a small hall, the sweet thunder of a no-holds-barred symphony-cum-chorale-cum-ballet, top Broadway names in a vast auditorium, or experimental drama in a storefront. It can be big-league sports in a mammoth stadium or indoor arena, or a Bluegrass banjo in a bare wooden hall. It can mean Las Vegas-type names and shows in a giant hotel or a neighborhood piano bar, or a lecture on a college campus; an evening in a dinner theatre large or small, rock bands of international renown and ear-splitting versatility, a quiet pianist in a late-night lounge, or anything in between. You can dance, sing, prance, shout, eat, drink, watch, listen, behave, misbehave, leave the kids or bring them along, mingle with the singles or whoop with the convention crowds, dine with the natives or cavort with the out-of-towners. The point is, in Atlanta at night, the city is the canvas and the palette; you're the artist.

There isn't any one special Atlanta-after-dark ambience, because there are so many Atlantas after dark. There was a time, perhaps twenty years ago, when you could catch a movie, dine in one of about ten adequate restaurants, see a show at a handful of downtown hotels, catch a night baseball game, and that was about the size of it. To see Atlanta after dark through the eyes of Atlantans themselves, you had to be lucky enough to be invited to an Atlanta home or club for dinner. No more, though; with the city's incredible explosion of affluence and commerce that began in the early 1960s came the big hotels, the nightclubs, the lounges and restaurants, the theatres and music groups, and the big names. And so now, even though to many native Atlantans a night out still means a quiet dinner in a good restaurant and perhaps a spot of dancing and a nightcap, the choices of what to do with yourself when the sun goes down are almost limitless. This section will tell you about many ways of diverting yourself after dark—from theatre to our music and dance scene, to nighttime sports and their aftermaths. There'll be a special section on fun things to do that don't seem to fit a neat category, too, and we'll suggest several evenings out that include cocktails, dinner, and shows.

One note: While we will suggest specific restaurants and nightclubs and lounges from time to time, especially on the organized evenings out, there'll be a more complete listing of restaurants and night spots later on, in a special section of this book, *DINING AND WINING*. And as we've said many times before, the local newspapers are the best sources of information on who's presenting what where on any given night. Big names sparkle in Atlanta every week, and this is the only foolproof way of keeping up with them. Have a good time!

EVENINGS OUT

Atlanta has an embarrassment of riches to choose from when it comes to painting the town. So much so, in fact, that we offer a few time-tested, ready-made evenings out for you to sample. These are evenings an Atlantan might put together for himself, and certainly they're proven favorites for "visiting firemen." Here you'll find evenings for glitter and glamour and big names, evenings up in the sky and under the streets, evenings as they might have been spent a century ago, and evenings as they'll be spent in Atlanta's soaring tomorrows. Some are expensive, some not so. Sample them, choose a few that suit you best, and by all means put together some of your own. These are just to get you started. When you do start building your own nights on the town in Atlanta, check the restaurants and lounges in the *DINING AND WINING* section.

ANTE-BELLUM EVENING OUT

Newcomers and visitors to Atlanta often have the idea that the city is a living museum, that white columns line Peachtree Street and restaurants are southern-fried chicken to the core, and night life is banjos, spirituals, and crino-line-whirling waltzes. Not so—the accent over-all is elegant, opulent, and upbeat. But there are still a few good places to eat, drink, and be merry with a bona-fide southern accent, even though just about the only white columns remaining on Peachtree Street belong to the sophisticated NBC radio and television affiliate, WSB-TV. This evening will introduce you to Atlanta the way she was almost a hundred years ago.

Aunt Fanny's Cabin, so the story goes, was once a slave cabin, and though it's been enlarged and refurbished many times through the years, it's still *the* place to go for authentic southern cuisine: fried chicken, ham, red-eye gravy, greens and fresh vegetables, and biscuits that float off your plate, plus a mean steak or two. The charm of the old building still remains, with well-re-created décor and touches, small black children bearing menu slates, and the like. It's the closest you're likely to get to the way we were. 436-9026.

To Aunt Fanny's: I-75 North, exit Mt. Paran, L Mt. Paran, R Rte. 41, L Spring Road—first left after I-285—L Campbell Road—second light—to Aunt Fanny's.

After dinner, kick up your heels in Atlanta as it really was in the roaring, brawling days when we were a brash young railroad town, in Underground Atlanta. Far more than just a tourist attraction, this old section of the city has been painstakingly restored to its former glory, all underneath the bridges and viaducts and streets that grew up over it and condemned it, once, to death. Here are the gaslights and cobblestone, cafés and saloons, warehouses and freight offices and banks, with a fine sprinkling of twentieth-century amenities such as several really good restaurants and many top-notch lounges, museums, and exhibits. Some of the lounges are extremely sophisticated and offer fine entertainment and dancing; try Dante's Down the Hatch for elegant jazz, Scarlet O'Hara's for Las Vegas-type entertainment, Ruby Red's Warehouse for rinky-tink banjo. Or, for a touch of Atlanta as she was, try the Apothecary Lounge (in a wonderful old drugstore), Muhlenbrinks's Saloon (one of the same name really stood here, once), or P. J. Kenney's Saloon, a remarkable re-creation of the area's most memorable saloon.

Or just wander at will and nip in wherever the music leads you. You could spend all night, and you well might.

From Aunt Fanny's: return to Rte. 41, L I-285 Greenville, I-75 South to Atlanta, exit MLK Blvd., two blocks to Underground Parking lot.

OMNI NIGHT

Atlanta's incredible Omni International complex is almost too vast and spectacular to comprehend in one visit. But it makes for a wonderful evening, or several, if you're determined to try everything. This is one night on the town you can do with the kids, if they've the stamina for it. Or, making a few substitutions, it can be as adult an evening as you're likely to find.

For starters, try a spin on the ice in the gigantic skating rink. Then, perhaps, have an early cocktail in one of the lounges of the nine excellent international restaurants that dot the complex. (Do stroll around first and see what's to choose from.) Have dinner in one of the restaurants, and follow with a postprandial stroll through the incredible European shopping bazaar and the glittering island of luxury shopping; they all are open till 11:00 P.M. Follow this with a first-run movie in one of the six theatres, or step next door to the Omni Sports Arena via a covered walkway and take in a Flames hockey game or a Hawks basketball game, if they're in town.

Top off the evening with a nightcap in one of the restaurants or lounges—you know the ropes by now.

Omni is on Techwood at Marietta Street—follow signs from points downtown.

SKY'S THE LIMIT

In Atlanta, it's entirely possible to spend an evening in the sky and never touch ground. Atlanta's great urban centers offer a wonderful variety of entertainment and dining among the stars, and for people who'd like to get a sense of the scope of this careening city, plus a feel of its heart and pulse, this evening can't be beat. It's sheer spectacle, from cocktails to nightcaps.

Start with an early cocktail or two at 590 West Peachtree, atop the Sheraton in Midtown. The décor is spare, contemporary, and dramatic, and makes a fine foil for the panorama of Midtown at twilight seen through the sweeps of glass surrounding you.

From downtown, north on Spring about one mile to Sheraton's parking garage. From north or south of city, I-85 to North Avenue exit. At exit, if heading south, turn left; north, turn right onto Spring. R Spring about ½ block to garage. Walk across bridge to hotel.

Next, slip down to the Sun Dial Restaurant, atop the stunning new Peachtree Plaza Hotel. This is truly the top of Atlanta, soaring some seventy stories above the city and accessible via an outside elevator. The tri-level restaurant and lounge is one of the city's very best; cuisine is traditional European-American with some lovely surprises, and impeccably prepared and served. And the view is unmatched anywhere in the South. You can have a predinner drink in the Sun Dial Lounge, which revolves slowly atop the whole thing, or a cocktail on one of a series of dramatic "Cocktail Pads" hanging dizzily out over the lake in the lobby. There are other good restaurants in the Peachtree Plaza, but this is a night for sky watching. 649-1400.

Directions to Peachtree Plaza: go south on Spring, to International Blvd., L into Plaza Hotel. Valet parking available.

Finish your evening in midair with a nightcap and show at Another World, the jewel in the crown of the new Atlanta Hilton Hotel in Atlanta Center, Ltd. Take another elevator to the glass-walled Eagle's Roost, at the very top; the view here is spectacular too, but hardly a match for the goings on inside. The room itself is visually stunning, and the sound-and-light pyrotechnics are simply not to be missed. Even on the clearest nights, you can shiver pleasantly through a man-made thunder-and-lightning storm that will make the real thing look tame by comparison. The entertainment is top-flight, too. It is unforgettable. . . . Another World. 659-2000.

To the Atlanta Hilton and Another World: north on Spring one block, R Harris, park on right; or walk from Peachtree Street exit of Plaza Hotel, turn L one block to Harris, R on Harris, two blocks to Hilton.

ALL THAT JAZZ

No Atlantan really believes that jazz is the special province of New Orleans. For many years, the best names in the business have come to town and enthralled audiences, and many of the local nighteries book jazzmen of all sorts, from Dixieland to big-band to cool. Rock may roar and symphonic music soar; pop may pound and folk flow like wine, but, in Atlanta, jazz goes on forever. This particular evening lets you sample three distinct jazz "sounds," with an extraordinarily good dinner to boot, and though it's a bit flung out, all true jazz buffs will find it rewarding.

The Keyboard Lounge, at 3861 Roswell Road, in Buckhead, is a superb place for a cocktail or so to start things off. Each evening from five to eight there's a glorious jazz fest to go with the drinks; it's a true *aficionado*'s hangout. This is where both Atlanta jazz musicians and visiting out-of-town artists gather. Whether they're just listening or sitting in, they give The Keyboard a special cachet all its own, and the shop talk is as fascinating as the music itself.

From downtown: I-85 North to exit Piedmont, L on Piedmont to Roswell Road, 4 miles, R on Roswell about one block; on right is The Keyboard.

For dinner and some of the best cool jazz in town, try Dante's Down the Hatch, in Underground Atlanta. Underground literally reverberates at night with music and jazz, much of it the café-Dixieland variety, but Dante's has wisely kept the superb Paul Mitchell Trio happy for years, and their elegant, low-key, inventive sounds draw customers by the hundreds each evening. Dante's dining room is a remarkable re-creation of an old sailing vessel, and the house specializes in simply marvelous fondues, cheeses, and wines. 577-1800.

Return on Piedmont to I-85 South, exit MLK Blvd., two blocks to Underground Atlanta Parking.

Tempted though you might be to linger at Dante's, you must not miss your nightcap stop at Pascal's La Carrousel Lounge, near the campus of the Atlanta University Center. This excellent establishment, part of what has been called the best totally black-owned motel-and-restaurant operation in America, has for many years attracted the nation's top jazzmen. There's no telling whom you'll be hearing when you go. Atlanta's jazz *cognoscenti* go regularly, though, so you'll want reservations for the late set. 577-3150.

To Pascal's from Underground Atlanta: continue on MLK Blvd., about 2 miles. You'll see Pascal's Motel. Park here. On right of motel is the lounge. Return to city by MLK Blvd.

Sports and After

In this city of Bobby Dodd, Pepper Rodgers, and Henry Aaron, the sporting life is a winner with tots, teens, middle-agers—everyone, in short, and their grandmother. And with four major-league teams in town doing their stuff at big-league Atlanta Stadium or the incredible, futuristic Omni Sports Arena, night sports proliferate the year 'round. These two evenings will help you wine, dine, and cheer both before and after in the Omni and at the stadium. As the man said, nothing will ever replace night baseball.

Omni night might start very early, with an exploratory spin on the giant ice rink in the stunning Omni International complex. Then drinks and dinner at one of the nine excellent international restaurants in the complex. Then drift over to the Omni Sports Arena via a covered walkway if the Flames are in town on the ice or the Hawks on the court. (Seasons are fall and winter.) Omni Box Office, 577-9600. Afterward, have a late snack or a nightcap in one of the aforementioned restaurants, and take a moment just to walk around and see the European shopping bazaar and the glittering luxury-island shops. The beauty of this evening is that it's all under one soaring roof.

I-85 South, exit Williams, R International to Omni. From south, take I-85 North, exit International, follow signs to Omni. For tickets, 681-2100.

A night-baseball or, rarer, evening-football game at Atlanta Stadium is one of the city's liveliest evenings, and you really ought to make dinner a light meal of the classic hot dog and beer (or Coke, as the case may be). 522-6375 for ticket information.

After the game, celebrate in Underground Atlanta in any one of the festive lounges and restaurants.

From downtown: Mitchell Street past State Capitol Building, L Memorial, R Capitol Avenue, to parking on right or in garage at Internationale Hotel. To Underground Atlanta: return on Capitol to MLK Blvd., three blocks to Underground Atlanta.

ONE-STOP EVENINGS

A favorite night out for Atlantans is simply drinks and dinner with a spot of dancing afterward. If you'd like an evening on the town that combines all three under one roof, the following restaurants are among those that offer good drinks, food, and dancing.

Ambassador, The, 3850 Roswell Road, N.E., 261-7171.

Château Fleur de Lis, 2470 Cheshire Bridge Road, N.E., 633-2633.

Crown Room, atop Colony Square Hotel, Peachtree Street at Fourteenth, 892-6000.

Daddy's Money, Prado Shopping Center, 5600 Roswell Road, 252-8686.

Diplomat, The, 230 Spring Street, N.W., 525-6375.

Gatsby's Restaurant, Atlanta American Hotel, 688-8600.

Harbour House Restaurant, Marriott Hotel in downtown, dancing in adjacent Cove Lounge, 659-6500.

Journey's End, 1180 Powers Ferry Place, Marietta, Ga., 424-8050.

Michael's Acropolis, 2391 Peachtree Road, N.E., 261-5262.

The Moorings Restaurant, 6700 Powers Ferry Road, 256-3667.

Smuggler's Inn, Powers Ferry Landing Shopping Center, 252-1021.

Stouffer's Top of the Mart, Atlanta Merchandise Mart, 688-8650.

Twentieth Century Limited, The Century Center Hotel, I-85 at Clairmont Road, 325-0000.

WORDS AND MUSIC

Atlanta loves theatre, and it's rampant, from the newest and most experimental productions in a downtown storefront to an all-out star vehicle in a creamy dinner theatre. Or the magnificent Civic Center to the no less elegant, if a bit more traditional, theatre performed by the fine repertory companies at the Alliance Theatre in the Memorial Arts Center and Atlanta's outstanding and long-standing Academy Theatre. And we love music, as evidenced by the crowds that turn out for the truly first-rate Atlanta Symphony Orchestra.

This section will tell you about the dramatic and musical events that have stood the test of time in Atlanta, and will endure. These are the organizations that have a permanent "home"—their own place to perform, with regularly scheduled seasons. It seems unfair to omit the several fine, small, new theatre companies that have sprung up recently; some of the city's most innovative and creative offerings emanate from them. But like most new groups, theatres struggle and often close their doors, and Atlantans have seen too many of their favorite newcomers quietly fold their tents and slip away. Again, the local newspapers carry a complete listing of current theatre in their amusements sections, and you'll find the best of the small and new featured there. Do, if you're a theatre buff, read those pages carefully to find some of Atlanta's very best drama.

As for musical organizations, we list here the ones that have homes and regular seasons. Some of Atlanta's most beloved musical groups present only quarterly or semiannual performances. These will be covered in the NIGHTTIME AND THEN SOME section of this *NIGHTTIME ATLANTA* portion of the book. The same goes for dance groups, lecture series, and other nighttime activities that are not to be missed but occur relatively infrequently.

Here, with the theatres and symphony, we'll suggest a

good and convenient place to dine beforehand, and a place for a nightcap afterward. We'll also give you box-office numbers. Reservations are strongly advised for all.

The Alliance Theatre, in the Atlanta Memorial Arts Center, has its own distinguished repertory company and presents a balanced mix of "experimental" and traditional dramatic fare. It's a first-rate company housed in a stunningly beautiful theatre, and has performances most week and weekend nights, plus a Sunday matinee, winter till spring. 892-2414. We'd suggest dinner beforehand at Brothers Two, in Colony Square, just across the street on the corner of Peachtree and Fifteenth streets, or at one of the restaurants at the sumptuous Colony Square Hotel, also in the Colony Square complex. We suggest the same two places for dinner before visiting the Atlanta Symphony and the Peachtree Playhouse. They're the best bets in the area for activities in and around the Arts Center. Afterward, if you're in the mood for a nightcap, drive out Peachtree about a mile. On the left, at 1776 Peachtree, is The Coach and Six, with a fine small lounge. A bit farther on, on the right, is Clarence Foster's, a tradition for after the theatre; and about two blocks farther out on the left in Harrison's, stunningly decorated in Art Deco-Victorian and one of the hands-down favorites with sophisticated young Atlantans. For parking at the Memorial Arts Center, drive just past the complex and turn left into the parking lot.

The Peachtree Playhouse, at 1150 Peachtree Street (about two blocks before you reach the Memorial Arts Center), is home to Atlanta's beloved Theatre of the Stars, and its winter play season is tops. Name performers and a wide variety of dramatic fare, from comedy to drama to musical to revue-type productions, make it one of the most popular and diverse groups in the city. 892-4110. For a bit of variety in your nightcapping, you might want to try one of the little lounges in the Sheraton-Biltmore, 817 West Peachtree Street. For the theatre,

you can park in the lot just next door to the Peachtree
Playhouse.

*Go south on Peachtree, R 5th Street, R into parking
lot.*

The Academy Theatre, at 3213 Roswell Road, in Buckhead, is a wonderment. It's one of Atlanta's oldest established theatres, and has consistently presented excellent
drama, with the emphasis on experimental and contemporary, without an "angel" or subsidization of any sort.
Director Frank Wittow is dynamic, sensitive, and a local
legend. The theatre is situated in a picturesque old church
and has its own fine repertory company, performing on
weekends mainly, so do check the papers for hours.
261-8550. For dinner beforehand, try Sidney's Just South,
on the right about a mile farther out on Roswell (small
but excellent); E.J.'s, in Cates Center (turn left into
Andrews Drive about a half block before you reach the
Academy)—or, for something big and glamorous, Brennan's famed New Orleans establishment is on West Paces
Ferry nearby.

*L at Peachtree-Roswell fork onto West Paces, one
block to Brennan's.*

For the theatre, you can park in the small lot adjacent
to the Academy, if you're lucky.

*To the Academy: north on Peachtree about 5 miles,
take Roswell Road fork at Peachtree and Roswell Road,
just a short distance to theatre on right.*

The Civic Center, near downtown at 395 Piedmont Avenue, is home almost every week to an internationally
known headliner and a wonderful variety of entertainment, from pop and rock concerts to drama to musicals to
opera to revues and variety shows. Here's where the real
stars shine, and it goes on practically all year long. Performers' engagements are frequently one night only, or at
best limited, so it's vital that you check the newspapers to
see who's in town the week you are. 523-1879. You're
close to downtown and all its fine hotel and motel restaurants, so you might want to dine in one of them, but a

great favorite with Atlantans is Gene and Gabe's, a small and exquisite little North Italian restaurant at 1578 Piedmont. It's a bit of a drive, but a straight shot back into the Civic Center and worth the trip. For a nightcap, try Underground Atlanta, Omni International, or perhaps the spectacular view from the Sun Dial at the top of Peachtree Plaza Hotel, or the popular Atlanta Hilton; our favorite is Another World.

The Atlanta Symphony presents a fall, winter, and early spring full of wonderful symphonic music in Symphony Hall at the Atlanta Memorial Arts Center, frequently with some of the most glorious names in music as guest conductors and artists. Conductor Robert Shaw often brings in full choral groups and dance companies for truly spectacular events—one of the best shows in town during the week, on weekend nights, and at Sunday afternoon performances. 892-2414. Afterward, imbibing is slim in the immediate area, save for the Colony Square Hotel and Brothers Two, but about a mile and a half north on Peachtree are The Coach and Six, Clarence Foster's, and Harrison's. All are fine. Symphony parking in the lot adjacent to the Arts Center. A note: Outstanding performers of all sorts, from musicians to mimes to rock groups to pop stars, often book Symphony Hall for one or two nights when the Symphony is dark. Check the papers.

The Fox Theatre, at 660 Peachtree Street, is one of the most spectacular structures in the country and is worth visiting just for a peek at its twinkling stars and drifting clouds, fantastic Moorish architecture, and elegant 1930s interiors. Closed as a movie palace now, with its future uncertain, the Fox is still home to wonderful one-and-two-night performances by the world's great names in rock, pop, jazz, ballet, opera, drama, and whatever. These performances are booked by individual groups, so it's well worth a flip through the newspapers to see who might be at the Fox while you're in town. By all means, cross the street to Salvatore's for dinner beforehand; it remains one of the city's very finest Italian restaurants, and Sal himself

has long since achieved legend status. The menu runs to
delicately prepared North Italian dishes, but ask Sal about
his specialties. Afterward, slip over to West Peachtree and
drive north till you come to the Sheraton-Biltmore for an
intimate nightcap, or try downtown at the gaggle of nighteries in Peachtree Center or the glorious Omni. (The Fox is
now on the National Registry of historical sites.)

*Fox: north on Peachtree about a mile from center of
town to theatre.*

The Omni, downtown at Spring and Marietta streets,
regularly books the likes of Sinatra, Dionne Warwick,
Count Basie, the international-biggie rock groups, entire
circuses, ice shows, and even the incredible Royal Lip-
pizaner Stallions into its futuristic sports arena. 577-6900.
For dinner before or after, or a nightcap, just stroll
through the covered walkway into the Omni International.
Several restaurants, at least one going strong all night, and
a myriad of clubs and lounges are here, along with the
most incredible world of shopping and entertainment you
ever saw. You simply don't need to leave the Omni complex for the best of dining, entertainment, and wining.
Park in the Omni parking lot.

*From Expressway follow signs to the Omni. From
Peachtree: R International to Omni.*

The Atlanta Municipal Auditorium, at 30 Courtland
Street, downtown, isn't much on looks, but for generations
it's been home to Atlantans seeking good entertainment,
and it still hangs in there with regularly scheduled performances by the best names in show business. Check the
papers. There simply aren't any truly good restaurants in
the area, so for dinner beforehand we'd suggest one of the
good downtown spots like the ones in the Hyatt Regency
Hotel, the Peachtree Plaza Hotel, and the Top of the
Mart—all in Peachtree Center; the elegant, futuristic eateries in the new Hilton Hotel in Atlanta Center, Ltd.; or
the good restaurants in the Marriott Motor Hotel, the
closest. Afterward, try Underground, the Omni, or the
soaring lounges atop the Hyatt Regency or the Peachtree

Plaza for a nightcap. Or back to the Marriott for some good music and dancing.

For parking at the Auditorium, south on Courtland, park in lots near Auditorium. They will be well marked.

ALL THIS AND DINNER TOO

It's a fact—Atlantans love to wine and dine, and they love theatre. So when the relatively new concept of dinner theatre slipped into town ten or so years ago, it quickly became a household word and a household favorite. Dinner theatres are great family places, depending, of course, on what sort of dramatic fare is being offered, and the idea of a good meal and an evening of comedy or drama all under one roof is appealing.

For years, the city had only one or two dinner theatres, leaning to substantial, if limited, cuisine and spritely, if less than Broadway-caliber, performances. But recently, with the upsurge in popularity of dinner theatres across the country (more than three hundred now), many intriguing dinner theatres have come to town, offering excellent and sophisticated menus and top-name performers.

Atlanta's dinner and cabaret theatres offer a great variety of moods, food, décor, and dramatic fare. You can go all-out elegant and star-struck in glossy Peachtree Center, downtown; Elizabethan and atmospheric in Buckhead; rustic and intimate in Marietta; or sharply satiric and wildly uptown-funny in Midtown. You can pelt the villain and pinch the wenches (gently) in a sixteenth-century English theatre restaurant, or catch a spritely revue in suburban northern Atlanta. All in all, the food, service, performers, and general ambience are good at each one, and sometimes outstanding. We'd advise reservations for all.

The Barn Dinner Theatre, at 1690 Terrell Mill Road, in Marietta, is Atlanta's most enduring dinner theatre, having delighted the natives for more than ten years now. Atmosphere is casual, intimate, and rustic, with real barn trappings and a young cast that is unfailingly appealing, handsome, and quite polished. The theatrical fare runs to light, popular Broadway-type offerings, and the buffet is ample and attractive. Tuesday through Saturday, buffet preceding the show. 436-6262.

Take I-75 North, exit I-285 West, exit Rte. 41, R Terrell Mill Road, R about ½ mile to Barn.

The Empire Suite of the Sheraton-Biltmore Hotel, at 817 West Peachtree Street, is home year 'round to the mordantly funny and long-cherished original revues presented by Atlanta's own Wits End Players. Nothing is safe from or sacred to this group, and the material is always singingly topical. Tuesday through Saturday, with a buffet beforehand. Also, there's a Tuesday matinee performance with a buffet preceding it, starting at noon. 892-2227.

From downtown on Peachtree, bear left at West Peachtree fork, about one mile, R 5th Street, L into Sheraton-Biltmore parking.

The Harlequin Dinner Theatre, at Piedmont-Peachtree Crossing Shopping Center, is a stunning reproduction of Shakespeare's Globe Theatre, with all the attendant timbering and trappings. Visually beautiful, it offers a talented young cast performing a good mix of Broadway-classic fare, with some Shakespeare every season. Shows run Tuesday through Sunday, with a buffet beforehand, and there are matinees with buffets on Wednesday and Sunday. 262-1552.

North on Peachtree to Piedmont 7 miles, L Piedmont a short distance, L into Center.

Manhattan Yellow Pages, located in the Omni Complex, is one of the sprightliest new additions to the nighttime dinner-cabaret theatre scene the city has had in many a year. A charming, talented, and electrically vibrant young troupe dispenses four absolutely first-rate revues nightly, each done in a fresh, innovative, and thoroughly professional manner. Dinners are ample, and good, too. Revues nightly except Sunday, and food service begins at 7:30 P.M. 581-0624.

The Midnight Sun Dinner Theatre, downtown in Peachtree Center, 577-5050, is the spectacular handiwork of the Center's architect, John Portman, and offers the city's most sumptuous setting, trappings, and views of downtown Atlanta to go with its productions. The fare is strictly big-time and glossy, as are the star performers who are brought in from Broadway and Hollywood for each production. The stage itself is worth the trip, as is the incredible Danish buffet served beforehand, courtesy of the incomparable Midnight Sun Restaurant, in the same complex. Performances are Tuesday through Sunday with buffets preceding, and there is a Sunday buffet and matinee as well as a Wednesday buffet-matinee. 577-7074.

Coming from north, exit Courtland, a few blocks to R International, one block to Midnight Sun parking on left. From south, exit International, 2 blocks to parking. You can walk across the bridge right into the theatre.

NIGHTTIME AND THEN SOME

Night-beat Atlanta is a kaleidoscopic scene. In addition to the Symphony, the various theatres, the evening sports, and the nights on the town already delineated in this section, there are countless other nighttime diversions you can dip into—some almost anytime you happen to be in town, others at scheduled times throughout the year. Special semiannual performances of dance, symphonic, and choral works, movies, lectures, slide presentations, concerts and recitals of all sorts . . . the beat goes on.

The ones we list here are only a few of the events crackling after dark in the city. This guide would be longer than *Gone with the Wind* if all were included. Again, check the Saturday and Sunday newspapers, the amusements pages of the dailies, and the Enjoy section in any current issue of *Atlanta Magazine* (on most newsstands). The Greater Atlanta Arts Council will also tell you what's popping during any given week if you'll call 892-8246.

Here are some additional and very special things to do in Atlanta under the stars.

MUSIC. During the summer months, *The Atlanta Symphony* presents a wonderful, lighthearted weekend series of pop-symphonic music at Chastain Amphitheater in Buckhead's Chastain Park, at Wieuca and Powers Ferry roads. It's a great family affair, with the stars blazing overhead and the night sweet in your nostrils. Many families take their own refreshments and munch and sip while they listen to music for a summer night. Call 892-2414 to see when.

The Atlanta Boy Choir is famous the world over and justly so. This stunning choir, made up of young boys whose voices have not yet changed, has performed in New York and Europe, and their annual European tours have received wide acclaim. Fletcher Wolfe, choir director, presents the boy choir in concert locally several times a year; it's a must if you're in town during concert time. Call 892-1908 to see when and where they're singing next.

The prestigious *Atlanta Music Club* has been a vital part of the arts in Atlanta for more than fifty years and has consistently—and often in the face of great odds—brought the city the world's truly great names in music. The club sponsors several series of fine performances, including individual artists and choral, operatic, and symphonic groups. Performances are staged at various locations in the city, including the spectacular Fox Theatre. Call 233-2131 to see what they've got on tap while you're in town.

Fine semiannual performances are also offered by the *Marietta Community Symphony*, the *Atlanta Pro-Mozart Society*, and the *Atlanta Concert Band*, to name only a few. Choral, concert, and opera companies abound. As do chamber groups. Again, check the newspapers or call the Greater Atlanta Arts Council, at 892-8246.

DANCE. There's been a virtual explosion of small, fine dance companies in the city in recent years. And though Atlanta usually gets one or more touring performances per year of such luminaries as the Robert Joffrey Ballet, the Alvin Ailey group, and even Fonteyn and Nureyev, the real, inventive electricity is out in the small halls and practice rooms of the city. Many are so small and new that they have neither permanent homes nor regular seasons, but their performances are always listed in the newspapers, so watch. Two of the city's oldest and best troupes are the *Southern Ballet* and the *Atlanta Ballet;* both offer regular performances several times a year, in one place or another. Their fare ranges from strictly classical to ultracontemporary, and their dancers are superb. Call the *Southern* at 233-5831 and the *Atlanta* at 261-9013 for wheres and whens. The *Decatur-DeKalb Civic Ballet* is fine, too. Phone them at 378-3388 for dates and places and such.

FILMS AND LECTURES abound all the time all over town. At the *Memorial Arts Center* there's midweek and weekend film and slide fare at both Symphony Hall and the Walter Hill Auditorium of the High Museum. These range from the immensely popular travelogs to films on major artists and their work to wonderful festivals of the golden oldies. Check the papers or call 892-2414. Hill Auditorium hosts frequent evening lectures, symposiums, and panels on anything from antiques to metaphysics to the women's movement.

The *Atlanta Public Library* has nighttime films and slide shows on just about anything under the moon. Special scheduled evening activities too, both at the main library, downtown on Carnegie Way, and the many suburban branches. These will be listed in the papers, or you can drop by any branch and pick up a free schedule of monthly activities. Or call 522-9363.

The *Atlanta Jewish Community Center,* at 1745 Peachtree Road, has a year-in, year-out program of evening activities, notable among them fine film and slide presentations on a staggering range of subjects. Check the papers or call them at 892-8246.

Fernbank Science Center is one of the greatest shows on earth—and off it—each Friday evening all year long, unless the weather is downright dire. The great observatory in the complex houses the largest telescope in the southeastern United States, and whether it's an eclipse, a moon walk, a comet, or just the awesome panorama of Atlanta's night sky, this is truly not to be missed. Great for children. The exhibit hall in Hodgson House, on the western edge of Fernbank Forest, is open until 10:00 P.M. Tuesdays through Fridays. Fascinating. Fernbank is at 156 Heaton Park Drive, N.E., and you can call 378-4311 for hours.

To Fernbank Science Center, take Piedmont Road north, R Ponce de Leon, follow to just before railroad trestle, and turn L Artwood, R Heaton, and follow signs.

Dining and Wining

For many people, visitors and residents alike, this is what it's all about. Atlantans who won't stir a limb to see a famous name in concert, take in a symphony, see a ball game, or go downtown just to see what's new and wondrous on the scene *will* go, and go regularly, to lunch or dinner at an old favorite or promising new restaurant. Visitors who don't really give a flip about the giant amusement complexes, the professional sports, the concerts or theatres or dance groups, *do* go in droves to dine out and sample the exotica in the city's clubs and lounges.

In this section, you'll find a representative sampling—and we *do* mean representative: there are *thousands* of places to dine and kick up your heels in the city. Here are the places Atlantans and visitors alike seem to favor when they set out to assuage a hunger pang, slake a thirst, or see a show.

There was a time when dining in Atlanta meant one of three things. Visitors to the city in the slumbering days before Atlanta caught fire and streaked into the rarefied atmosphere of the country's major cities might dine at a handful of old, established restaurants around town: an elderly French café, a couple of placid steak houses, and a group of those honey-and-lard-basted establishments known as professional southern. Atlanta residents seeking companionship and sustenance gave dinner parties, or they went to the club; there were few other options.

But, for the past couple of decades, with the quickening pace of the city; the swelling influx of visitors, conventioneers, and bright out-of-towners; and the rich stream of money pouring into the city from all over the world, dining has flourished along with the rest of the good life in

Atlanta. And today, in the last half of the supercharged seventies, eating has come of age in Atlanta as it has in few other American cities. Visitors and residents alike can sample at will from hundreds of types of cuisines in hundreds of restaurants, ranging from traditionally good steak houses, through the much-improved (if still professional) southern establishments, to almost every variety of ethnic eatery on the face of the earth. Some are enormous, glossy, and frankly legendary; others small and elegant; still others brassy, funky, and fun. It's simply not true any more that you have to go to Chicago for a decent steak, or Manhattan for quenelles. Whatever you're hungry for, in whatever setting you fancy, at whatever price you wish to pay, Atlanta has it.

The following list is not intended to be an unbiased, critical, and comprehensive representation of eating out in Atlanta. That task would be impossible, given the space in this book. What you'll find here is a sampling of those restaurants whose popularity with visitors and residents makes them particularly worthy of note. For this reason, we urge you to consult the excellent dining-out section in each month's *Atlanta Magazine*, which you'll find on most newsstands. This is a fine and far more comprehensive roundup of what's available to munch in the city. The Atlanta Convention and Visitors Bureau puts out a fine annual booklet called *What's Up in Atlanta Restaurants and Lounges*, and you can get a copy by calling them at 659-4270, or writing or dropping by the Visitors Center in Peachtree Center just off Peachtree Street.

But, for the nonce, we'll tell you about these favorites, and we'll give you addresses, plus phone numbers to call for reservations and information. We urge that you call ahead; the recent change in Atlanta's liquor laws, allowing for the sale of drinks on Sundays, is going to change days and operating hours significantly in almost every case, and this new information is not available to us at the time this book goes to press. In addition, we'll indicate if each restaurant accepts major credit cards, with the inclusion of code letters MC. And we'll indicate whether each is expensive, moderate, or inexpensive by coding each E, M, or I. A reservation is a good idea at any restaurant listed, on any given day. Lunch is a bit looser, but reservations are still a good idea in the biggies.

A note: Most large hotels have at least one restaurant that stays open till the wee, small hours, and some go all night. You can always find a dawn's-early-light bite downtown.

The Abbey, Piedmont Ave. between North & Ponce de Leon aves., 876-8532. MC. M. Housed in a wonderful old restored church and done up in elegant, medieval trappings, The Abbey features, among its other fine traditional dishes, especially good Filet Mignon Henri IV, Pompano Belle Meunière, Oie Roti. The wine list is excellent. Dinner only.

Anthony's, 3190 Piedmont Road, N.E., 233-7129. MC. E. Anthony's is in an authentic plantation house, built in 1797 and moved brick and board to its present location. The décor is charming, definitely not overdone, as in so many "southern" restaurants, and the menu includes beef and excellent seafood, as well as a good selection of French dishes. Good wines and "southern" drinks, if you insist. Dinner only.

Aunt Fanny's Cabin, 375 Campbell Road, Smyrna, 436-9026. MC. I. If you must eat southern style, do it here. Aunt Fanny's is built around an authentic and carefully restored slave cabin, and serves southern-style cooking that will not shame its legendary namesake: succulent fried chicken, country ham, flaky biscuits, tender greens and vegetables, and desserts, such as pecan pie, that Sherman never quite managed to destroy. Small black boys in southern costume—whatever that is—recite the menu in a cheerful singsong, and have been part of the show since the place opened. Dinner only, except for Sunday lunch.

Benihana of Tokyo, 2143 Peachtree Road, N.E., 355-8565. MC. M. This spectacular, oversized Japanese temple is a wonder architecturally. Every piece of wood, nail, shingle, strip of flooring, and whatever, was made in Japan and shipped to Atlanta, to be assembled by Japanese workmen imported for the task. The warren of rooms inside is charming and beautifully done, and the antics of the specially trained, acrobatic Japanese chefs make it a showplace. Cuisine is artfully and speedily minced and diced and cooked at *hibachi* tables and served in work-of-art arrangements. Beef, chicken, and seafoods are specialties, and the most popular dishes are combinations of all. Lunch and dinner.

Brennan's, 103 West Paces Ferry Road, N.W., 261-7913. MC. M. The Atlanta branch of New Orleans' famous favorite brings its legendary ambience and Creole cookery to town in a lovely setting of mirrored walls, greenery, velvet, and crystal chandeliers. Delicate fish and seafood are specialties, with oysters topped with a vast array of Creole sauces particularly good for appetizers, and eggs every way under the sun, are the stars of the famous Saturday and Sunday breakfasts at Brennan's. The stunning sazerac cocktail is justly famous too. Lunch and dinner.

Bugatti, Omni International Hotel, One Omni International, 659-0000. MC. E. This elegant Italian eatery under the megastructure of the futuristic Omni complex proffers some of the lightest and most succulent North Italian cuisine in the city. The menu is especially notable for its seafood appetizers—a great favorite is the mushrooms and scallops marinated in a light, olive-oil-based sauce—and wonderful entrees with the accent on veal and seafood. A sauteed trout with mushrooms and artichokes recently moved the author's party nearly to tears of joy. Beef, too, if you must. Lunch and dinner.

Clarence Foster's, 1915 Peachtree Road, N.E., 351-0002. MC. M. This artfully chic little watering hole began life as one of the premier spots for the smart young to lunch and meet for cocktails and dinner, and it still remains almost painfully "in." The patrons—almost all regulars—are clubby in the extreme, but you can't fault

their high good humor and gloss. The décor is wonderful:
a long, brass-railed bar and a greenhouse dining room,
glassed in to protect diners from the elements, as lushly
planted as a rain forest. The menu runs from simple—
splendid hamburgers and a marvelous spinach salad—to
unusual and elegant, and late-night eggs Benedict after the
opera or theatre is a tradition. Lunch and dinner.

The Coach and Six, 1776 Peachtree Road, N.W., in
Midtown, 872-6666. MC. M. Holder of several *Holiday*
Magazine awards for excellence, this consistently fine restaurant features classic American dishes, with steaks, veal,
and lamb a specialty. Seafood is infallibly good too. In
fact, the author never had a bad or even a so-so meal here.
The décor resembles that of a smart midtown Manhattan
restaurant; the lounge is dim, lush, and a favorite hangout
for the city's advertising and P.R. types. An enormous
mural features a montage of local celebrities. Lunch and
dinner.

The Coromandel, Colony Square Hotel, Colony
Square, 892-6000. MC. E. This may be the most spectacular restaurant in the entire city. The Coromandel
has been cited by designers from all over for its
magnificent contemporary décor, which is light-years away
from stark, bare "modern." Magnificent appointments and
a stunning Coromandel screen, from which the restaurant
takes its name, give it a rich Asian ambience. The two-
story glass wine rack alone is worth a trip to see, but the
classic French cuisine is very good indeed, and the service
impeccable. Lunch and dinner.

Cross Roads, 1556 Peachtree Street, N.E., 875-6575 or
875-2288. MC. I. The Cross Roads has been a favorite for
Atlanta families since it opened its doors, nearly thirty
years ago, and remains so today. There's a truly staggering
variety of seafood at extremely affordable prices, ranging
from the enormous fisherman's platter to stuffed flounder,
shrimp, lobster, scallops, oysters, and just about every fish
that ever cruised the seven seas. The whopping heaps of
miniature shrimps, either boiled and served with sauce or

delicately fried, are a special favorite. Children are welcome and seem to love it. Lunch and dinner.

The Crown, Colony Square Hotel, Peachtree at Fourteenth Street, N.E., 892-7960. MC. M. This beautiful dining room sits atop the 27-story Colony Square Hotel in Colony Square, with sweeping views of the city's skyline to the south and a sea of trees to the north. There are entertainment and dancing in the evening, though no cover or minimum, and the buffets give the lie to the old saw that nobody ever got a good meal out of a buffet line. These are superb, sumptuous, and one of the best bargains in town. Sunday brunches of heroic proportions are a specialty. Lunch and dinner.

The French Restaurant, Omni International Hotel, One Omni International, 659-0000. MC. E. A truly luxe French restaurant in the incredible Omni complex, with unusual selections of classic French cuisine served to perfection in a charming garden environment. Besides the food, which is probably the best and most innovative French in the city, it's the little touches that set The French Restaurant apart: exquisite menus, fresh bouquets on the tables, beautifully designed napery; and there's nightly entertainment, too, plus uncommonly attractive private dining facilities for larger groups. There are many French restaurants in the city; if you've time for only one, make it this one. Lunch and dinner.

Herren's, 84 Luckie Street, N.W., downtown, 524-4709. MC. M. Herren's is said to be Atlanta's oldest restaurant, and it's still one of the best. Long a lunchtime favorite with Atlantans who work downtown, it does a brisk dinner trade too—and is one of the few downtown eateries not connected with one of the vast new hotel complexes. Proprietor Ed Negri is just about as legendary as his restaurant, and is on hand greeting lunchers and diners regularly. Seafood is a specialty—you can choose your own lobster from the tank in the lobby—and the wonderful planked seafood platter is an Atlanta tradition. Lunch and dinner.

Hugo's, Hyatt Regency Atlanta, 265 Peachtree Street, N.E., Peachtree Center, 577-1234. MC. E. Hugo's has an unusual menu of classic Continental food, with exquisite crevettes Lorenzo and legendary pastries. The décor is unusually well-done and quietly stated contemporary. Perhaps the most popular dish on the dinner menu—and deservedly so—is the flaky, tender beef Wellington. Lunch and dinner.

Joe Dale's Cajun House, 3209 Maple Drive, N.E., in Buckhead, 261-2741. MC. M. The Cajun House has a clientele of regulars who are convinced they discovered it—and they guard it jealously. The author is one of them. It's a funny, unpretentious little restaurant on the outside, with wonderful antique toys and dark paneling inside, and an inspired kitchen that produces Creole delicacies without peer in the South. Seafood is always good, especially the oysters, and the veal is touched with heaven. There's an oyster stew, which comes walloped with shallots and spinach, that's superb; a fine, hearty gumbo; a legendary salad that no one but the staff knows how to make; and what the author considers to be the best fried oysters in the world. All entrees come with plates of garlic potatoes, "dirty rice," and wonderful red Creole beans. Go—but don't tell everybody about it. Lunch and dinner.

The Magic Pan, Lenox Square Shopping Center and Cumberland Mall Shopping Center, Lenox, 266-8424; Cumberland, 432-3115. MC. M. These cheerful, country French restaurants abound in fresh flowers, antiques and old prints, and polished copper, and serve tender, incomparable crepes wrapped around just about everything that's edible. There are other French delicacies on the generous menus too, but the crepes are really what make the Magic Pan restaurants worth leaving home for. Brunch, lunch, dinner, dessert, late supper.

Mimi's, Omni International complex, One Omni International, 688-5900. MC. E. Mimi's is an absolutely spectacular restaurant, featuring "natural California" décor: cocktail tables made from glass-topped giant tree trunks sawn in half, rioting plants, lots of wood and leather, and real, "textury" things. The menu leans to classic American and traditional Continental offerings, with an accent on simple things—beef, poultry, seafood—perfectly prepared, seasoned, and served. There are some unusual and usually good dishes, abounding in natural seasonings and herbs. Mimi's has perhaps the city's most unusual appointments. Lunch and dinner.

Midnight Sun, 255 Peachtree Street, N.E., in Peachtree Center, 577-5050. MC. E. Just about this author's favorite of all when the occasion is out-and-out splendid. An enormous menu with the accent on Scandinavian, but the classic Continental dishes are superb, too. Wines and sauces are impeccable, and the service is quiet and attentive. The décor is dramatically contemporary, centered around a massive fountain, with flaring bronze arches and a cave-quiet air of lush intimacy. Lunch is a great Atlanta favorite, but it's dinner when this superb restaurant really shines. An exceptional chef and kitchen staff. One of the city's favorite and most dramatic lounges for cocktail-hour unwinding, too. Lunch and dinner.

Nikolai's Roof, Atlanta Hilton Hotel, Courtland and Harris streets, N.E., 659-2000. MC. E. They call it the crown jewel of the Hilton, and it has a rich, intimate Middle Eastern atmosphere, enhanced by opulent appointments and an air of romantic, Czarist-Russia intrigue. An outstanding menu and a spectacular floor-to-ceiling wine vault. Do try it; it's not your ordinary meat-and-potatoes fare. Dinner only.

Nino's, 1931 Cheshire Bridge Road, N.E., 874-6505. MC. M. On the outside, Nino's is a small, square, plain white stucco building that looks as if it might have been a laundromat at one time. On the inside, you'll find one of the great North Italian dining experiences in the city. Starting on a shoestring with a small handful of regulars who gathered to pay homage to the peerless cookery, Nino's has blossomed in the past few years into one of Atlanta's most treasured of eateries, and has begun to attract national note. Atlanta's Italian-American community dine here regularly—always a good sign—and its ambience is that of a cheerful, hilarious, friendly, very Italian bistro in New York or, perhaps, Italy. The veal and seafood dishes are done with a deft hand, and Nino's sauces are, hands down, the best in the city. If you're a special friend, or very lucky, the chef might whip you up something not listed on the formidable menu. Dinner only.

Petite Auberge, 2935 North Druid Hills Road (Toco Hills Shopping Center), 634-6268. MC. M. A suburban shopping center may seem a rather strange setting for one of the city's best French restaurants, but there sits Petite Auberge, looking for all the world like the little French country inn it takes its name from, and dispensing impeccable French food with a fine, delicate hand. The dining room is handsome and elegantly appointed, the service is simply fine, and the food infallibly good. Veal is exceptional, as are the seafood dishes, and there's a lamb dish done with rosemary and Lord knows what else that is little short of sensational. Lunch and dinner.

Pittypat's Porch, 25 International Boulevard, downtown, 525-8228. MC. M. Pittypat's is, as you'll gather from its name, southern to the core, but a bit more uptown than Aunt Fanny's country place. The décor is charming, with its rocking chairs and authentic southern antiques, and there's a fine collection of ante-bellum memorabilia. You can get traditional southern cooking here, but you'll find good traditional American and Continental fare too. A special highlight is the lavish cocktail buffet at happy-hour time, which is beautiful, bountiful, and a meal in itself. And there's the ageless, heart-tugging charisma of Graham Jackson's piano music, playing songs of the South, old and new. Diners old enough to remember Jackson playing "Goin' Home" on his accordion as Franklin Roosevelt's funeral train moved slowly north from Warm Springs, Georgia, will be compelled to shed a tear or two, but his magic is by no means limited to the older crowd. Dinner only.

The Pleasant Peasant, 555 Peachtree Street, N.E., 874-3223. MC. M. A small and superb traditional menu, painstakingly prepared and lovingly served, in one of the city's most unusual and well-done small restaurants. The Peasant is a converted drugstore tastefully gotten up with bare bricks, plants, and cheerfully shining brassware. The patrons, like the staff, are largely young and with it, but you could run into anyone, from any age group and life-style. Dinner only.

Reggie's, Omni International complex, One Omni International, 525-1437. MC. M. Reggie's is perhaps the newest, best, and most authentic of the crop of British-type pubs flourishing in Atlanta, partly because owner Reggie Mitchell is an Englishman himself and of distinguished lineage (General Cornwallis, we hear). Situated on the lobby level of the Omni International Hotel, Reggie's robust, charmingly Victorian pub serves up hearty British fare, with such specialties as steak and kidney pie, wonderful beef, Cornish pasties, and Scotch eggs. Informal and great fun. Lunch and dinner.

Salvatore's, 669 Peachtree Street, N.E., 881-9190. MC. M. Sal has one of the city's first authentic North Italian restaurants, and this author still thinks it's the best in town. Light, delicate, perfectly spiced and sauced veal, beef, and seafood dishes are featured, with veal the province of a special genius in Sal's kitchen. The restaurant is small and dark and properly atmospheric, and if genial, dinner-jacketed Sal is around, ask him if there's something special cooking up that evening. He just might whip you up something that isn't on the menu, that will make you think you've died and gone to heaven—an Italian heaven. His Caesar salad should be immortalized. Lunch and dinner.

The Sun Dial, Peachtree Plaza Hotel, Peachtree at International Boulevard, N.W., 649-1400. MC. M. A stunning, tri-level restaurant atop the world's tallest hotel, in Peachtree Center, with a traditional menu excellently prepared; silky, unobtrusive service; and an incredible view of the city from all directions. You can take the outside elevator up seventy stories to the top if you're hungry and brave enough. Have drinks in the Sun Dial Lounge, revolving slowly above the restaurant level, or in the Sun Dial Balcony, a series of cocktail "pads" overhanging the whole affair. Lunch and dinner.

Trader Vic's, Atlanta Hilton Hotel, Courtland and Harris streets, N.E., 659-2000. MC. M. Long a legend in San Francisco, and in New York, where it has held forth for years at the Plaza, Trader Vic's has come South and brought its fabled Polynesian ambience and appointments with it. The menu features international cuisine, with a strong emphasis on Polynesian dishes: succulent seafoods done with fruits and spices garnered, as it were, from the seven seas. Trader Vic's drinks are hands-down show stealers, being served in coconut shells and Lord knows what else, whopped with all manner of exotic fruits and flowers, and laced with enough spirits to pole-ax a sailor on shore leave. Shades of Somerset Maugham! Lunch and dinner.

Sports and Specials

You've sampled the electricity of Atlanta under the sun, tasted the drama of Atlanta after dark. And we've only just begun. What remains is a kaleidoscope, a grab bag if you will, of intriguing things to do all year 'round—things to watch, participate in, laugh at, swear at, cheer, boo, dance to, sing along with, celebrate. These are the "specials": special sports on a giant scale; special sports to do on your own, on a smaller scale; special, once-a-year events to enthrall you. If daytime Atlanta and nighttime Atlanta have left you with a nagging taste for just a little something more, you'll find it here . . . in *Sports and Specials*.

SPORTS YOU DO

For all its sports-watching mania, Atlanta is a city of doers. Movers and shakers. Golfers, tennis players, swimmers, cyclers, boaters, skiers, riders, skaters, hikers and climbers, and wilderness lovers. If there's a participant sport we don't have, we will soon. And there's probably a club devoted to it.

Participant sports are by no means the province of the establishment or the local equivalent of the Four Hundred. The City of Atlanta Parks and Recreation Department has put golf, tennis, swimming, cycling, baseball, football, and basketball within reach of virtually anyone who wants to play. Privately owned establishments take up the gap for boating, skiing, horseback riding, ice skating, and wilderness sports. Private clubs offer fine tennis and golfing; if you know a native who's a club member, some of the nation's finest play in both sports is available to you in Atlanta.

And if you don't, don't fret. The following listings will cover just about anything you and your family might want to do. Except for the rare and really vicious cold spells Atlanta can dish out in January and February, you'll find Atlantans outdoors playing everything all year long. Except the swimming season (a bit shorter) starts usually in early May and lingers till late September, but many hotels have indoor pools, so if you simply must get wet in January, there's probably a way.

The following sports are open to the public with no exceptions. We haven't listed clubs and organizations devoted to sports because most, of course, are for members only. But not to worry. We doubt if you could work through the list in a month of Sundays.

GOLF

The City of Atlanta Parks and Recreation Department maintains seven fine public courses within the city. Of them, the following three are especially challenging and popular. So much so, in fact, that we're listing numbers to call for starting times. Given Atlanta's linksomania, it's a very good idea, indeed. If you'd like the names and locations of additional courses, which are placed around the city so that there's golf in all geographical locations, call the Recreation Division of the City of Atlanta Parks and Recreation Department at 658-6381.

Bobby Jones Golf Course, Atlanta Memorial Park, 384 Woodward Way, N.E., 355-9049. Named for the master himself, and an extremely popular course. 18 holes.

North Fulton Golf Course, Chastain Memorial Park, 216 West Wieuca Road, N.E., 255-0723. One of the most challenging courses in the South, public or private. 18 holes.

Piedmont Golf Course, Piedmont Park, Piedmont Avenue at Fourteenth Street, N.E., 872-9129. 9 holes.

TENNIS

If tennis is a national mania, in Bitsy Grant's town it's mass hysteria. At last count, there were more than 150 public courts in Atlanta, maintained by the Parks and Recreation Department. They're full every day—and some at night—all year 'round. Courts in public parks are usually first-come-first-serve, and peak hours are early morning, noon, and late afternoon and evening in the case of lighted courts. In the summers, when the kids are out of school, you might want to try a very early-morning start, but school season clears things out a bit and you can usually find a court in the mornings, and afternoons before three. All are well maintained, and players are usually courteous about limiting their sets, so you probably won't have to wait long anywhere. Proper tennis footwear is a must at most facilities.

The following hotels and motels have unusually fine tennis and racquet sports facilities, if you happen to be a guest:

The Atlanta Hilton Hotel, in Atlanta Center, Ltd., downtown at Courtland and Harris streets, N.E.

Dunfey's Royal Coach, downtown on I-75, at Howell Mill Road exit.

Hilton Inn-Airport, south of Atlanta, across from the airport.

Marriott at Perimeter Center, I-285 and Ashford-Dunwoody Road, north of the city.

Radisson Inn Atlanta, at Chamblee-Dunwoody Road and I-285, north of the city.

Terrace Garden Inn, on Lenox Road, northeast of downtown area, off Peachtree Road.

In addition, the following three public tennis complexes are centrally located in Midtown and the Buckhead area, and offer unusually fine tennis facilities:

Bitsy Grant Tennis Center, Atlanta Memorial Park, 2125 Northside Drive, N.W. Thirteen Tenniko courts, ten Laykold courts, one practice court. Lighted. Tennis center and clubhouse. This is one of the finest tennis facilities in the Southeast, so you'll probably have a wait. It's worth it.

Chastain Memorial Park (North Fulton), Wieuca Road, Powers Ferry Drive, and Lake Forrest Road, N.W. Nine lighted Laykold courts.

Piedmont Park, Piedmont Avenue and Fourteenth Steret, N.E. Thirteen lighted Laykold courts.

Again, if you'd like the names, addresses, and phone numbers of additional tennis facilities in the city, call the Recreation Division of the City Parks and Recreation Department at 658-6381.

SWIMMING

For an inland city, Atlanta has a lot of wet natives. There are private pools, neighborhood-association swim clubs, country clubs, college and university pools, the excellent and ubiquitous YMCA and YWCA pools, hotel and motel pools, a scattering of beaches at nearby lakes, and about one million backyard pools of the inflatable, cool-the-kids-and-wash-the-dog variety. And then there are the public swimming pools operated by the City Parks and Recreation Department. Your hotel or motel is likely to have a pool of its own, perhaps even an indoor swimming hole, but should you want to branch farther out, the public swimming pools are excellently maintained, spotlessly clean, and as popular as a popsicle (or a cold Coca-Cola) on a hot summer day. The pools maintained by the Parks and Recreation Department usually accommodate the kids, so they open after school's out, in early June, and close after Labor Day. Call the Recreation Division of the City Parks and Recreation Department at 658-6381 to find out about public pools.

Other swimming holes are apt to stay open as long as it's warm—which can mean late September in Atlanta. Before you leave home, you might check with your hotel or motel about their policies; otherwise, pack your bathing suit only in the good old summertime.

There's sand-beach swimming within a comfortable distance of wherever you are, too. Spectacular *Stone Mountain Memorial Park* has, in addition to its other attractions, four enormous white sand beaches complete with bathhouses and good restaurants and snackeries.

To Stone Mountain from downtown: I-85 South, exit I-20 East, exit I-285 Greenville, exit Stone Mountain Freeway, Athens, exit Stone Mountain Park.

And *Lake Lanier Islands*, about thirty-five miles northeast of Atlanta via I-85 and Georgia 365, has a marvelous white sand beach on its vast blue lake front, with a bathhouse and restaurant adjacent. (Plus about a million other outdoor things to do. This is a great favorite with Atlantans.)

To Lake Lanier Islands: I-85 North, L 365 Gainesville, exit #2 Friendship Road, turn left and follow signs to Lake Lanier Islands—about 4 miles from the expressway.

BICYCLING

Atlanta has a wealth of glorious, tree-lined vistas that would make marvelous bike rides—and do, for natives who know the territory and the traffic laws and patterns. But marked routes and paved trails for riding are lamentably scarce in the city. And while just about every other Atlantan has a bike and rides regularly, *we do not recommend that a visitor hop on a cycle and take off at random*. The traffic is just too murderous and the terrain too steep for unplanned jaunts.

But there *is* good cycling in the city, courtesy of both the Parks and Recreation Department and the excellent Southeastern Bicycle League, and if you're a serious cycler, you can manage some of the most beautiful and challenging cycling to be had in these parts.

Three city parks have marked bicycle routes that are fine for children and novice riders. They're fairly gentle, not too long, and well marked so you don't get lost. They are:

Joseph E. Brown Park, Ormewood Avenue and Pendleton Street, S.E.

Stanton Park, 213 Haygood Street, S.W.

Williams Park, Jackson Parkway, N.W.

In addition, the city of Decatur (just to the east of Atlanta) and the city of Atlanta, with the help of the federal Bureau of Outdoor Recreation, have put together a total of eighty miles of marked bicycle trails, stretching from the Decatur city limits through Piedmont Park and Ansley Park in Northeast Atlanta and circling back to the starting point. The portions in Piedmont Park (a vast and beautiful city park on Piedmont Avenue at Fourteenth Street) and Ansley Park, a charming, winding old residential area just across Piedmont Avenue from the park, are especially popular and make fine, if somewhat hilly, cycling. Follow the arrows, but do be careful. Traffic, especially in Ansley Park, can be suicidal. Child riders should stick to Piedmont Park.

Both these areas are especially stunning in the spring and fall. If you'd like to have a map route of the whole bloody eighty miles, write or call the City of Atlanta Parks and Recreation Department, 260 Central Avenue, S.W., Atlanta. 658-6381.

Best bets for serious cyclers—and that means experienced and trail-toughened—are the wonderful series of bike rides sponsored by the Atlanta-based Southeastern Bicycle League. These occur almost every weekend, year 'round, with a really experienced leader taking bikers on long, prerouted rides in various parts of the city and the surrounding countryside. *Not* for novices; fifteen miles is not uncommon. But glorious if you're good. The league puts out a monthly publication called "Free-Wheelin'," which is available in just about all bike stores throughout the city for $.30. You'll find a multitude of bicycle stores in the Yellow Pages of the Atlanta phone directory, and the publication will have a list of rides and tours occurring while you're here, plus the leader's phone number for information: dates and places to meet, how long the ride is, and what sort of terrain you'll be covering—in short, the works.

If you're a serious cycler, you'll probably have brought your bike along. Bike rentals are scarce in Atlanta. But you can rent good ones at Name Brand Bicycles, 4502 Roswell Road, N.W., near the Wieuca Road crossing. Call them at 255-2467.

BOATING

If you've driven through many of Atlanta's residential sections, from modest to magnificent, you've probably noticed almost as many boats tethered in garages and backyards as you have automobiles. In the spring, summer, and fall, Atlantans take to the water like lemmings, in just about everything from dinghies to destroyer-like cruisers. Nearby Lakes Lanier and Allatoona afford fine boating for boat owners, but the pickings are slimmer for those who'd like to rent a craft and set sail. It can be done, however, and it's a fine way to pass a balmy day.

Lake Lanier Islands, a beautiful and spotlessly maintained 1,200-acre resort on Lake Sidney Lanier, less than an hour's drive from the city, has, in addition to cottages, golf, tennis, beaches, horseback riding, and other sybaritic under-the-sun activities, a multitude of boats to rent by the day, the weekend, or the week. The wandering blue lake, with its hidden coves and estuaries and islands, is a lovely place to lose yourself for a spell, and is big enough so the private boat owners, the renters, the sailors, and the motor-craft folk don't splash on each other's toes. The big story on Lake Lanier is houseboating, and Lanier Island Rentals will rent you houseboats that sleep six or eight. They're stocked except for towels and napery and food, and a better way to spend a summer weekend hasn't been found yet. Call them at (404) 945-6731. Or write ahead to Box 356, Buford, Georgia 30518, and they'll send you a brochure and all information.

Lanier Island Rentals will also rent you canoes, kayaks, spritely little motorized pontoon boats, and various sail craft. You're pretty much on your own after you've cast off, so don't attempt to set sail unless you know safety rules and how to operate your craft. Lake Lanier is enormous and can be crowded and quite squally. You wouldn't take an automobile on a city expressway without knowing how to drive, and the same holds true on the lake. Houseboats are the exception; no experience is necessary.

To Lake Sidney Lanier: I-85 North, L 365 Gainesville, exit #2 Friendship Road, turn left, follow signs. About 4 miles from expressway.

Stone Mountain Memorial Park has wonderful boating on its huge blue lake and will happily rent you a craft during the late-spring, summer, and early-fall months. Sailing is especially popular here, or you can rent rowboats, canoes, and fun little electric "whaleboats." Not so large and crowded as Lake Lanier, Stone Mountain Lake is probably a better bet if you're a real novice or have very small children along. And there's a wonderland of family things to do at hand when you finally dock.

To Stone Mountain from downtown: I-85 South, exit I-20 East, exit I-285 Greenville, exit Stone Mountain Freeway, Athens, exit Stone Mountain Park. About 17 miles from downtown.

You can, of course, rent a boat and trailer in the city and take it to one of the nearby lakes, but renting at the water's edge, with all gassing and servicing attended to, makes more sense if you have limited time. Some boat dealers have sail and motor craft for rental, along with trailers and accessories; you can find them in the Yellow Pages under "Boat Dealers."

FISHING

Georgia is a fisherman's paradise, but it's not easy to wet a hook in the city. A note to the Georgia Game and Fish Commission, at 270 Washington Street, S.W., Atlanta, Georgia 30334, will get you information on what's biting best where in the state, and if you've time, you should give it a try. Lake, river, and salt-water fishing is paradisical in these parts.

If you'd like to indulge in a bit of fishing closer to home, you might try one of the following public fishing lakes:

Cedar Grove Lakes, 6285 Cedar Grove Road, Fairburn, Georgia. 964-3001.

Rainbow Ranch, Highway 20, in Cumming, Georgia. (404) 887-4797. Trout's a specialty, and you get free bait and tackle.

Chuck Sexton Lake, 4070 Demooney Road, College Park, Georgia. 964-3131.

Lake Lanier Islands, an hour to the northeast at Buford, Georgia, has among its many other outdoorsy splendors, three well-stocked, terraced trout ponds in natural woodland settings, where you can fish by the pound. Fine eating, whether you cook it yourself or have it cooked up and served with your favorite side dishes on the premises, just minutes after you land it. Bait and tackle are free.

Lake Allatoona, a large lake to the northwest of the city, has some fine fishing. Especially notable is the bass fishing in the Victoria Landing area of the lake, off Georgia Highway 205 south of Canton. To learn about water and fishing conditions, give a call to Bill Hodgins Bait and Tackle Shop in Canton. They can supply more explicit directions, too. (404) 479-4788. You'll want to take your own tackle and bait, and you can put in at Victoria Campgrounds, in Victoria Landing.

Two nearby fish camps will rent you boats and motors and give you directions so you can reach the landing area by water. They are Little River Camp, about thirty minutes from Victoria Landing (404) 974-6200, and King's Camp, ten to twelve miles from the landing (404) 974-6710.

And if you really haven't much time, just drive west till you hit the Chattahoochee River (it's impossible not to) and drop a line from a gentle bank near the bridges. You'll have lots of company.

It's a must that you check with the Game and Fish Division of the Georgia Natural Resources Department about a fishing license. Call them at 656-3523 for all information, including where to pick one up. They generally aren't any problem.

HORSEBACK RIDING

Atlanta is a horsy town. The elegant Shakerag Hunt is here, along with the annual steeplechase, which draws throngs of tweedy fans every year to picnic in splendor, with crystal and silver and fresh flowers, off tailgates and Rolls Royce roofs. Then there's the annual Hunter-Jumper Classic, the annual DeKalb County Sheriff Posse Rodeo, and a host of shows for horses in every category, from the slender, princely Arabians to the tough, agile little quarter horses. Stables and riding academies abound, too; thousands of Atlantans own their own animals and board them in stables scattered throughout the city.

It's tougher if you're simply in town and want to ride a

horse. Since so many stables and riding academies offer boarding, training, and instruction but no rental animals, visitors who want to spend an afternoon or so on horseback will have to work a little. Your best bets, short of bringing your own horse, are the following:

J-Rad Stables, less than an hour from the city at spectacular Lake Lanier Islands, has day and evening trail rides on the wooded islands set in the lake, and a shaded pony ring for youngsters. There's a good stable on the premises, with trained personnel to see that your mount matches your skill. Call them at 945-6164 or 945-7307.

To Lake Lanier Islands: I-85 North, L 365 Gainesville, exit #2 Friendship Road, turn left, follow signs. About four miles from expressway.

And if you're inclined to drive a distance for some of the most beautiful riding trails in the Southeast, you won't want to miss *Peaceful Valley Farm,* Rte. #1, in Clarkesville, Georgia. The trail rides are glorious, and the owners will take beginners as well as the experts. Call 1-947-3300.

To Peaceful Valley: I-85 North, L Rte. 365 Gainesville, exit #6, Rte. 129, L Rte. 129, R Rte. 75 toward Helen. At Indian Mounds, turn R #17, L #255 at Old Sautee Store—runs into Rte. #197. Peaceful Valley is on your right.

Some of the area's many stables and academies do offer rides by the hour; policies change. If you're dead set on exploring the riding situation further, the best thing would be to call a few of them (they're listed under "Stables" or "Riding Academies" in the Yellow Pages) and ask if they have rental mounts available.

Rafting and Wilderness Sports

Nobody knows quite how it got started. But rafting and inner-tubing down the Chattahoochee River are as much a part of an Atlanta spring or summer as blossoms and baseball. There's hardly a weekend from late April to late September when the gentle stretch of river from Morgan Falls Road to Paces Ferry Road doesn't look like some fantastic, ragtail flotilla straight out of Kurt Vonnegut. *Everybody* rafts, young and old, entire families, entire college fraternities. . . . It's not unusual to see as many as 15 or 20 rafts or tubes connected, bobbling downriver like a berserk island. An attached inner tube bearing refreshments is the perfect accessory for your raft; and even if you haven't time to get your own bottom wet, a drive out to the bridge at Paces Ferry Road at the Cobb-Fulton counties line is worth it, just to see the show.

If you'd like to give it a try, you can rent a raft from Lanta Rent-a-Raft on U.S. 41, south of I-285, next to World of Frames. Call them at 432-5417.

You can put in at Morgan Falls Road off Roswell Road, off I-285, or at Johnson Ferry Road off Roswell Road, off I-285. Another popular point of embarkation is a county recreation area on Powers Ferry Road, off I-285. Take out at U.S. 41, or West Paces Ferry Road at the Cobb-Fulton border. It's a mild, pleasant two or three hours, with looming, wooded palisades along the way and a few gentle rapids just to keep you awake. Picnic lunches, liquid whatever, and shorts or bathing suits with a cover-up for sun are musts.

If you've seen the movie *Deliverance* and you *still* want to canoe a Georgia river, you must be serious. We assume you're at least good enough to handle your boat over some fairly hairy rapids. The section of the Chattahoochee delineated above makes a good afternoon's run; above Morgan's Falls, things get wild and you *must* be expert. If you want to give it a try, you can rent a canoe or kayak from High Country, Inc., at 6300 Powers Ferry Road, N.W., 255-4684.

For real wilderness lovers, *Southeastern Expeditions, Inc.*, at 666 Edinboro Road, N.W., offers Chatooga River rafting and guided whitewater trips, both day and overnight, via rafts and canoes. These are for knowledgeable woodspeople. The Chatooga, where *Deliverance* was set and filmed, can be murderous, and is not to be played around with. These trips are licensed by the U. S. Forest Service and led by really experienced leaders, so you'll be in good hands. *Southeastern* also has instruction and outfitting in backpacking, canoeing, kayaking, and climbing. 355-3550.

Skating

Blades or wheels, it's all one in Atlanta. Roller skating has always been a popular sport, especially for families, and with the advent of the Atlanta Flames, ice-skating rinks are mushrooming all over the city. The joy of Atlanta's rinks is that they're open all year long, many of them until late in the evening, and the city returns the favor in droves. Some of the larger ice rinks are surrounded by glossy hotels, galleries, shops, and other amusements, and a whirl around the ice can be a pleasant interlude in a day spent on the premises. Others are situated in their own buildings around the city. So whether you're a wobbly-ankled novice or just missed the Winter Olympics by a hair, there's a rink in Atlanta that's just your speed and size.

Roller Skating

Greenbriar Skating Center, 3850 Stone Road, S.W. 344-7619.

Playland Roller Skating Center, 4405 Buford Highway, N.E., Chamblee, Georgia. 457-8811.

Rainbow Roller Rink, 5480 Brown's Mill Road, Lithonia, Georgia. 981-3121.

Ice Skating

Omni International Ice Arena, in the magnificent Omni International complex, downtown at 100 Techwood Drive Viaduct, N.W., is simply an experience unlike any other. This giant rink is ringed by the shopping bazaars and luxury shopping islands, the host of fine restaurants and lounges, and the countless other splendid diversions of this unique pleasure dome. A trip here to skate is going to take you all day and into the evening, because you simply can't go to the Omni and just skate. You have to stay and do everything. Pro shop and snack bar. 688-5993.

Belvedere Ice Skating Rink, at 2939 Wesley Chapel Road, in Decatur, is one of the city's most popular and established rinks. 289-1234.

Ice Land of Atlanta Skating Rink, at 2400 Herodian Way, boasts an Olympic rink with hockey, speed, figure, and recreational skating, and is where the luminous Atlanta Flames hold their practice sessions. 432-0143.

Parkaire Olympic Ice Arena, in Parkaire Shopping Mall, at the intersection of Lower Roswell Road and Johnson Ferry Road, has an Olympic-sized rink, instruction, and a pro shop. 973-0753.

There are other rinks, both for ice skates and for roller skates, in the city; these are just the highlights. A glance at "Skating" in the Yellow Pages will glean others for you.

Skiing

It's not surprising, of course, that many Atlantans can water ski soon after they can walk. With Lakes Sidney Lanier and Allatoona so close by, and a climate that's good for getting wet except for about five months of the year, water skiing is a local mania.

But the big surprise story in Atlanta is snow skiing. The Atlanta Ski Club is one of the nation's largest and schedules regular jaunts not only to the resorts nearby in the mountains of northern Georgia, North Carolina, and Tennessee, but to the fabled snowgrounds of Aspen, Vail, Switzerland, Austria, Germany, and even Chile. Ski shops abound in the city, and it's simply not safe any more to assume that the winter tans sported at holiday parties were acquired in the Caribbean. Fully half probably came from the peaks.

Visitors in town for a few days or a week can bone up or keep in touch all year long now, thanks to the excellent and exhilarating *Vinings Ridge Ski Area*, in the historic little village of Vinings, just to the northwest of the city. The all-weather runs can put skis under novice and expert alike, in June as well as January, and it's a great way to spend a morning, an afternoon, or an evening with your family. You can rent whatever gear you need in the rental shop, receive certified instruction, or just schuss or sitzmark to your heart's content, depending on your degree of skill. There's an excellently stocked ski shop, too, plus an atmospheric little restaurant and lounge, and ski movies are offered most nights. An intriguing family thing to do, and one that's catching on with Atlantans who don't want to wait till the snow flies. Do try it.

I-285, exit Paces Ferry Road Vinings, turn right if heading north, left if south. Continue on Paces Ferry Road, less than one mile, turn right at ski sign— Boulevard Hills Road. Follow signs to ski area, less than a mile. From downtown: I-75 North, exit Mt. Paran, L Mt. Paran, R Rte. 41 about one mile to L Paces Mill Road. Follow straight about 2 miles (becomes Paces Ferry Road) to L Boulevard Road; follow signs to ski area.

SPORTS YOU WATCH

Atlanta is sports crazy. Always has been, always will be. Long before the city went major league, the crowds at beloved, scruffy old Ponce de Leon Park (now, alas, defunct) roared and bellowed in the soft summer nights to the enthusiastic, if dubious, artistry of the Atlanta Crackers. Since 1893, autumn Saturdays have been studies in cheerful mayhem as the Georgia Tech Yellow Jackets take Grant Field. Suicidal stock-car races are not new; the dusty oval out at Lakewood Park once reverberated with shrieking engines and bloodthirsty fans. Friday-night wrestling has long been a sociological phenomenon worthy of close attention from Margaret Mead. And in this town of Bobby Jones and Bitsy Grant, golf and tennis matches are as natural to natives as a cold swig of Coca-Cola on a hot summer day.

Then, in 1965, the Milwaukee Braves came to town and became the Atlanta Braves, and the majors had a beachhead in Atlanta. The Atlanta Falcons followed, and then the Hawks, and then the Atlanta Flames began to burn up the ice at the Omni, and there was no doubt in any rabid sports fan's mind that the city had kept its appointment with destiny.

And now, on just about any given day the year through, somebody somewhere in the city is kicking, hitting, dribbling, skating, racing, riding, and, not infrequently, scratching and biting. And on just about any given day, a happy crowd is watching all of it. Here's a rundown on the best and most popular of the many sports that are thriving in Atlanta.

Atlanta Stadium, at 521 Capitol Avenue, S.W., is home to both the Atlanta Braves and the Atlanta Falcons. The Braves season starts in April and goes until World Series time; tickets at the Stadium. The Falcons season is October through December; tickets at the Stadium, or call 588-1111. Parking in the Stadium lot is ample. The Stadium Club is a posh, glass-enclosed eyrie with a fine view, drinks, and food, if you're lucky enough to know someone who's a member. The traditional hot dog and beer around the seventh inning or at half time is probably just as much fun.

The Omni, at 100 Techwood Drive Viaduct, N.W., hosts the Atlanta Hawks and the Atlanta Flames. The Hawks dispense fine basketball from October through March; tickets at the Omni, all SEATS locations, or call 577-9600. The fabulous Flames take the ice October through March also; tickets, again, at the Omni and SEATS outlets. The Omni boasts a huge, multi-level parking lot just across the street from the arena. There's an Omni Club for members, similar to the Stadium Club, and an incredible wealth of eating, drinking, and merry-making in the Omni International, adjacent to the coliseum via covered walkway.

Georgia Tech has crackling good football, courtesy the legendary Yellow Jackets at Grant Field, corner of Techwood and North Avenue, from September to December; call 894-5447 for ticket information. Parking is a bit iffy, strung out as it is along side streets bordering the field. A bus to the corner of North Avenue and Spring Street brings you within easy walking distance of things. Afterward, you might want to stroll back across the North Avenue viaduct to the Varsity Drive-In, or up to glittering 590 West at Stouffer's Inn, nearby at 590 West Peachtree, for a drink and some music in the glass-enclosed lounge atop the building.

Atlanta International Raceway, near Hampton, off I-85, twenty-four miles south of Atlanta, is home to some of the hottest and most hair-raising stock-car action in the South. The season is spring through early fall, and you can see the country's best drivers competing in such events as the Atlanta 500 in March and the Dixie 500, a NASCAR Grand National Championship, in August. A.I.R. holds the city's record for attendance at a single event—some eighty thousand screaming, sunburned, totally happy people. Tickets through SEATS, or call 946-4211.

Road Atlanta, at Flowery Branch, Georgia, near Gainesville, is a sports-car track par excellence. The action is international, and the track hosts such events as CAN-AM racing and the American Road Race of Champions. Spring through fall finds roaring crowds, incredibly sophisticated and exotic autos, and the likes of Paul Newman, who has dropped in to race on a number of occasions, unannounced but definitely not unrecognized. Tickets at the gate, through SEATS, or call 523-7922.

Polo matches are played every Sunday at 3:30 P.M., May through October, at the polo grounds on Johnson Ferry Road, just across the Chattahoochee River bridge. The Atlanta Polo Club, founded in 1968, fields about twenty-five players, and they're good indeed. This princely sport is a hands-down Atlanta favorite. No tickets are necessary.

Wrestling in Atlanta is, was, and ever shall be. The hallowed Friday-night matches at the Municipal Auditorium, Courtland and Gilmore streets, downtown, have been running for years now, all year long, and more incredible mayhem you'll never find anywhere else. Things get under way about 8:00 P.M. and feature the Georgia state professional champion every week and the world heavyweight champion once a month. There are such goodies as women's matches, too, and a battle royal that has ten (count 'em) wrestlers in the ring at one time. Call 523-6880 for tickets and information, or pick up a ticket at the box office.

SPECIALS

Somewhere in Atlanta, on just about every day, there's
something special going on. Fairs, flea markets, parades,
festivals, tours of anything and everything, concerts, sporting events—you name it and Atlanta has a group that's
probably celebrating it right at this moment. Many of
these occasions are annual events—days and weeks that
Atlantans have come to cherish and count on. If you're
lucky enough to be in town while one of the city's annual
happenings is occurring (and it's hard *not* to be), you're
in for a treat. There's a European-holiday air to the city
when we're having a party for something, be it the Fourth
of July, the Metropolitan Opera, the ubiquitous watermelon, or a giant Christmas tree. And your whole family
will love every minute of our special events.

There are a wealth of annual specials occurring in the
city in each given month. In the interest of space econ-
omy, we've compiled a selected list of the ones that have
wide appeal and are an ongoing tradition in the city. You
can find scores of others in the newspapers. And while
most of them occur each year during a given month,
weeks and days change from year to year; so a riffle
through the Saturday and Sunday newspapers is vital for
exact dates and times. Also, the Georgia Bureau of Industry and Trade's Tourist Division publishes an excellent bi-
ennial listing of goings on all over the state, including
Atlanta, that's extremely comprehensive. You might want
to write for one at P. O. Box 38097, Atlanta, Georgia
30334. Or call 656-3590.

Finally, we'd like to mention the wonderful Ringling
Brothers Circus, which comes to town each winter at the
Omni, as does the spectacular Ice Capades and/or Holiday on Ice. Dates and months simply can't be firmed up
ahead of time, so we can't tell you which winter month
they'll be in town. Watch the newspapers carefully.

FEBRUARY

The Atlanta Boat Show is a wonderful week of everything nautical, from dinghies to enormous floating pleasure domes just under the Onassis class, plus everything to
accessorize all of it; comely hostesses, door prizes, the
works. It has been an Atlanta tradition for many years.
Check location in local papers.

MARCH

The Atlanta Hunt Meet and Steeplechase, in nearby
Cumming, Georgia, is one of the city's most hallowed
events. Fine riding and jumping, flashing silks, mounted
marshals in hunting pinks, and a general air of discreet
English revelry. Subscribers and VIPs may attend a lavish
tent breakfast and a dress ball; general ticket holders pack
a lunch and eat on blankets on the grass. Wear your best
tweeds, and beg or borrow a station wagon; it's the tailgate
lunches that make the show. You'll see everything from
paté and champagne served from heirloom silver and crystal, fresh flowers atop cars, and snowy linens to Levi's and
peanut-butter sandwiches. It's big-league horsemanship all
the way.

*From downtown: I-85 North to I-285 Interchange, L
on I-285 to North Fulton Expressway (I-400), R I-400
to Ga. 20, L Ga. 20 (Buford exit) to Ga. 19 (where 20
dead-ends), L Ga. 19 to Ga. 141, L Ga. 141 to Steeplechase turnoff on right.*

The Atlanta 500, at Atlanta International Raceway, in
nearby Hampton, is stock-car racing at its hair-raising best.
Take a lunch, a blanket, binoculars, and ear plugs.

*From downtown: I-75/I-85 South past Hapeville exit,
bear R on 41, continue on 41 about 23 miles to Hampton, R Hampton and follow signs.*

St. Patrick's Day Parade, downtown Atlanta. Wonderful floats and lots of foolishness, plus marching bands,
pretty girls, balloons, majorettes—the works. Is there anybody who doesn't love a parade? Green is not *de rigueur*.

Parade route downtown: stand on Peachtree Street near Peachtree Center and you're bound to enjoy the whole thing.

APRIL

Atlanta Dogwood Festival, all over the city for one glorious week in early April, is Atlanta at its most beautiful and hospitable. Timed to coincide with the incredible snowstorm of dogwood that clouds the city in the spring, this is a head-spinning week of gala festivities that include a spectacular Grand Parade down Peachtree Street, the crowning of the Dogwood Queen and presentation of her court, balls, street dances, concerts, fashion shows, arts and crafts of every variety all over the city, and sports events. It's a week you're not likely to forget. There are bus tours of the loveliest sections of the city, and you'll see flower power at its best. By all means, take part in some or all of the city-wide activities built around it if you're here. (The papers will be full of it, so watch daily and pick your activities.)

Egleston Tour of Homes, benefiting the Henrietta Egleston Children's Hospital, opens some of the city's most elegant and gracious homes for one or two glorious weekends in April, when the dogwood and azaleas are at their absolute best. This is the *grande dame* of Atlanta's many home-and-garden tours, and features houses both opulently traditional and innovatively contemporary. The papers will tell you how to get a ticket, and hostesses at each residence will guide you through.

Masters Golf Tournament, in Augusta, Georgia, isn't an Atlanta event, but we usually carry on as though it were. This *crème de la crème* of the golf world lures so many Atlantans to Augusta that Atlanta is practically deserted during its last weekend. Tickets are scarcer than hens' teeth, but if you're lucky enough to wangle one (and can find a place to stay in Augusta), you won't want to miss it. It's not a bad trip if you want to drive over for a day (about 180 miles), but you must have a ticket to watch.

To Augusta: straight on I-20 East; follow signs.

Stone Mountain Easter Services and Easter Egg Hunt. This can, of course, occur in March, depending on when Easter falls. Whenever, it's an inspiring and beloved Atlanta tradition. Services are held just at sunrise on the brow of the giant granite mountain, with massed choirs and triumphant music—truly glorious. Take a coat; it's cold on the mountain at dawn. The following Easter-egg hunt for children is tradition too, and thousands of ours turn out for it. Why not yours?

To Stone Mountain from downtown: I-85 South, exit I-20 East, exit I-285 Greenville, exit Stone Mountain Freeway, exit Stone Mountain Park.

MAY

The Arts Festival of Atlanta, in Piedmont Park, has been going on since the mid-1950s and is one week in spring when no Atlantan plans to go out of town. This week-long, outdoor affair not only has acres of art in all media displayed in rows beneath the lacy green trees, but there are special demonstrations of every craft imaginable, dance and theatre and choral groups and bands every evening, plus wonderful examples of sculpture, photography, crafts, and whatever is beautiful that can be created by human hands. Some of the art is superb and some is not, but all is for sale. And as a people-watching opportunity, it's without peer.

To Piedmont Park: Piedmont Road is 3 blocks east of Peachtree; follow north 2 miles to Piedmont Park on right.

The Atlanta Golf Classic. Held each year at the beautiful Atlanta Country Club, this tournament brings shining names in golfdom from all over, and offers a fine, fat purse to further brighten things up. Tickets sell out early, so watch the papers to find where you can get them.

To Atlanta Country Club from downtown: I-75 North, exit I-285 Greenville, exit Riverside Drive (sec-

*ond exit), turn left, follow to Johnson Ferry Road at
traffic light, turn left, follow signs.*

The Great Chattahoochee Raft Race, run each year
from Morgan Falls to the West Paces Ferry bridge over
the Chattahoochee, is a wonderful piece of spring madness
whose origins are clouded in the mists of time. All you
need to know is that if it can float, you'll see it on the
Chattahoochee on race day. Literally hundreds of craft—
rafts, technically, but you should see what some of the en-
trants can do with a lowly raft—bobble downriver, decorated with lavishness, ingenuity, or both. It *is* a race, and
there *are* winners, but competition seems beside the point.
The spectacle is the thing. The West Paces Ferry bridge is
a good watching point, but there are spots along the banks
all up and down the river. A county recreation area on
Powers Ferry Road, off I-285, affords good watching too.
Join in. You can rent rafts.

*Directions to one good vantage point: follow above
directions to golf tournament but stop on Johnson
Ferry bridge over Chattahoochee River. You'll have lots
of company.*

The Metropolitan Opera comes to town each May for a
week, and the result is genteel mayhem. This treasured annual visit goes back a long, long way, and has become as
much a social event as a celebration of the world's best in
opera. The Atlanta Civic Center is crowded each evening
with lucky ticket holders, dressed in their no-holds-barred
finest: gowns that languish all year in closets come out for
the Met, and you'll see ruffled tots, snowy-haired dowagers
in the family jewels, white-tied gentlemen, and anything
in between. Opera parties abound all over the city; indeed,
some wise Atlantans always schedule a week of their vacation during the Met's stay. Serious music lovers rarely
bother about what they wear, but everybody else does. It's
see and be seen at its most flagrant and glorious. Tickets
are usually sold out for all performances, but the Want
Ads during Met week always have some for sale, and our
classical-music stations have a ticket-exchange broadcast at

regular intervals during the day, so listen in. You may luck out. Or you can *try* the box office, 523-1879.

To *the Civic Center, at Piedmont and Forrest avenues: 3 blocks east of Peachtree, downtown.*

The Stone Mountain Classic Arabian Horse Show, at Stone Mountain Memorial Park, presents a shining fleet of these incomparable aristocrats showing their colors—and their riders' expertise—each May. Breath-takingly beautiful. Stone Mountain is the scene of many fine horse shows the year through; watch the papers or get hold of a copy of the Georgia Bureau of Industry and Trade Tourist Division's invaluable little booklet. They're all listed there. We told you how to get one in the introduction to this section.

To *Stone Mountain from downtown: I-85 South, exit I-20 East, exit I-285 Greenville, exit Stone Mountain Freeway, Athens, exit Stone Mountain Park.*

JULY

The Fourth of July affords some explosive high jinks in Atlanta. Here's a sample.

The Salute to America Parade, sponsored by WSB-TV, is the granddaddy of all Atlanta parades, and carries out its patriotic motif with literally miles of lavishly decorated floats, bands, majorettes, dignitaries, visiting stars, clowns, horses—everything, in short, to remind you what this country has come to in its short lifetime. Get yourself a cold drink and a curbside seat; it's Disney World marching.

Parade Route: right down famous Peachtree Street; good vantage point near Peachtree Center.

Fireworks spectaculars are just that on an Atlanta Fourth of July. Crowds gather from miles around at sundown to watch the heavens bloom and boom with hours of fantastic color, and the kids of all ages wriggle, gasp, and applaud. Two of the best are held at Lenox Square and at Stone Mountain. Take your pick, but go early; traffic in these areas is incredible.

To *Lenox Square: I-85 North from downtown, exit*

Lenox Road, turn left, follow to Lenox Square Shopping Center on left. To Stone Mountain: see directions for Arabian horse show, just above.

Watermelon Day at the State Farmers' Market is a full day's celebration of that most splendid of fruits, the ripe, red, Georgia watermelon. Stalls and rows and acres and miles of melons from the finest farms in Georgia. Pick a ripe one and dig in. There are bands, personalities, all sorts of live entertainment, and a stomach-boggling watermelon-eating contest for the kids. It's a down-home Georgia summer on a gigantic scale, and great fun.

To the Farmers' Market: I-85/I-75 South, follow I-75 South, exit Frontage Road (large sign says "State Farmers' Market"). Turn left and left again into market.

SEPTEMBER

The Atlanta Antiques Show, at the Civic Center, is the largest and most lustrous of the hundreds of antiques shows and fairs that go on in the city. These are the genuine articles—thousands of truly splendid (and costly) pieces, ranging from fine furniture from all periods to exquisite porcelains, crystal, silver, accessories. Whatever is fine, old, and beautiful, you'll find here. It's always crowded and a great Atlanta favorite; the entire creamy Northside turns out for the show. Wishers and lookers are welcome. If you want to buy, best bring your decorator and a great deal of money.

To the Civic Center: Piedmont and Forrest avenues, downtown, 3 blocks east of Peachtree.

Fashionata is the original creation of the omnipresent Rich's Department Store and is so far out of the ordinary fashion-show category that it has simply become an event, nearly as elegant as the Met. You'll see the very best and newest from the world's top couturiers in a framework of spectacular music, choreography, and superb showmanship. *Fashionata* has a different theme each year, but all are as spectacular as a Broadway production. Watch the papers for announcements of location and ticket information. (Yes, Rich's *will* sell you the creations you see.)

The Powers Ferry Crossroads Fair and Art Festival, near Newnan, Georgia, is one of the oldest and largest of the fairs and festivals that spring up like goldenrod in a Georgia autumn. You can browse or buy all manner of arts and crafts, watch demonstrations of same, take in a wonderful variety of on-the-spot live entertainment. Sample some of the South's best country cooking, poke around for antique and "jonque" bargains; in short, have a glorious time on a balmy fall day. Do go. As we said, there are hundreds of fairs and festivals and shows in Georgia this time of year. Get ahold of the ubiquitous Bureau of Industry and Trade Tourist Division's booklet.

Directions to Powers Ferry Crossroads: take I-85 South to Newnan and follow signs.

OCTOBER

The Scottish Festival and Highland Games, in a sylvan meadow at the foot of the mountain in Stone Mountain Memorial Park, is just about the most fun you can have on a fall weekend. Many of Georgia's original settlers were Scots who came down from the highlands of the Appalachian Mountains, and their kin and clans carry on the heritage with stirring highland games (ever seen a caber being tossed?), dances, parades, and bagpipe music. Kilts worn, of course. The massed marching pipe bands will give you cold chills, and you can bring a lunch or buy authentic Scottish goodies on the premises. (Shortbread is one thing, but haggis is another, altogether.)

To Stone Mountain: see under May.

NOVEMBER

The American Road Race of Champions, at Road Atlanta, in Flowery Branch, Georgia, near Gainesville, is a super biggie sponsored by the Sports Car Club of America, and is *the* place to be for sports-car buffs. The purse is big, the cars exotic, and the crowds incredible.

*From downtown: I-85 North to Flowery Branch, L
Flowery Branch exit and follow signs.*

The Dixie 500 Auto Race, at Atlanta International
Raceway, in Hampton, near Atlanta, is another biggie, but
for stock cars. Some of the best drivers in the business are
always there, and the crowd is worth watching even if you
don't know a cam shaft from a carburetor.

*Directions to A.I.R. From downtown: I-75/I-85 South
past Hapeville exit, bear right on 41, continue on 41
about 23 miles to Hampton, right Hampton and follow
signs.*

The Lighting of the Great Tree, each Thanksgiving
night, is a local tradition that has lifted hearts and spirits
for many years. It takes place on the multistory glassed-in
bridge that connects two portions of Rich's Department
Store downtown, and when the enormous evergreen tree
on the very top blooms into light, each successive tier of
the bridge comes alight and alive with massed choirs singing carols, amplified so that the street crowds can hear.
Truly lump-in-the-throat stuff.

*Park in Rich's Parking Garage on Alabama Street or in
the Deck Parking on Spring Street across from Rich's.*

DECEMBER

The Nutcracker Ballet, a joint production of the
Atlanta Symphony and the Atlanta Ballet, has been enchanting our young and young-at-heart for many, many
Christmas seasons now. It usually takes place on the four
days just after Christmas at the Civic Center (or perhaps
the Fox Theatre—check the newspapers) and is as much a
part of an Atlanta Christmas as egg nog and Santa Claus.
Don't miss it if you're in town, especially if you have
youngsters in tow. (Watch local papers for location.)

The Peach Bowl, Atlanta's own postseason college bowl
game, is usually played in late December. Check the
papers. There's a wonderful, noisy parade down Peachtree
Street beforehand, complete with floats, and some of the
nation's best college talent competing. (Usually at
Atlanta-Fulton County Stadium. Check local papers.)

Out of Town

If you have a day—or perhaps a weekend—to spare while you're visiting, there's no better way to spend it than exploring the countryside around Atlanta. Within an easy day's drive, the blue-shawled mountains of the Blue Ridge loom to the north, studded with spare, pretty little mountain towns and villages; arts and craft shops that are not, perhaps, as glossy as the ones you'll find in town but far longer on charm and authenticity; historic sites and recreational areas; lakes, creeks, and rivers; and the ancient, dreaming spell of these, the oldest mountains on earth. In the spring when the rhododendron and the mountain laurel spread the blue hills with their frothing blossoms, the Blue Ridge Mountains are unforgettable. And in the fall, when the wildfire of autumn flames on peaks and in hidden valleys, they can steal your breath away. Winter frosts them with snow, and summer breathes sweet and cool on them. Atlantans count the Blue Ridge Mountains among their civic treasures, and rightly so. We can get there and back in a comfortable day, if we're of a mind. And thousands of us do.

Also to the north, only an hour or so out of the city, is the water wonderland of Lake Sidney Lanier. Countless Atlantans have cottages and homes on this wandering, island-studded blue lake, and countless others spend days, weekends, and entire vacations in the vast, idyllic world of Lake Lanier Islands, where they camp or stay in comfortable cottages, golf, boat, swim, picnic, ride horseback, fish, or just shake the city off their souls.

Just an hour or so to the south of Atlanta, in the rich, rolling farm country of middle Georgia, history and nature

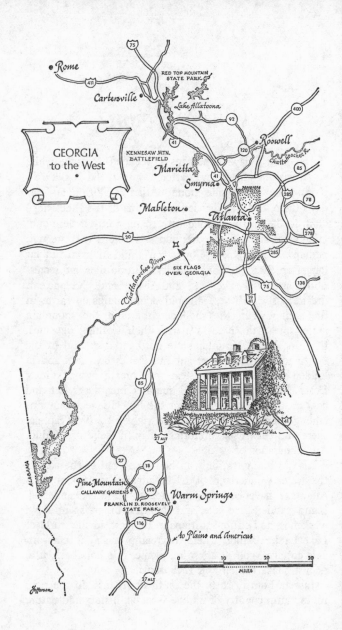

GEORGIA
to the West

Rome

Cartersville

RED TOP MOUNTAIN
STATE PARK

Lake Allatoona

KENNESAW MTN.
BATTLEFIELD

Marietta

Smyrna

Mableton

Roswell

Chattahoochee R.

Atlanta

Chattahoochee River

SIX FLAGS
OVER GEORGIA

ALABAMA

Pine Mountain

CALLAWAY GARDENS

FRANKLIN D. ROOSEVELT
STATE PARK

Warm Springs

to Plains and Americus

Jefferson

0   10   20   30
MILES

live easily and magnificently together with the incredible gardens and recreational facilities of Callaway Gardens and the beloved, much-visited Little White House, occupied by Franklin Roosevelt when he was President. Warm Springs, where he regained much of his health, is here too, as is the charming, completely restored little village of Hamilton—an incredible bit of loving and authentic restoration.

And to the east, the South of our gentle ante-bellum days comes vividly alive in Madison, Georgia, where immaculate white columns and giant old oaks dream much as they did in the days before the wind of the Civil War swept through Georgia and changed her face once and for all. Madison is a living, breathing treat for lovers of history, architecture, and antiques.

So, after you've seen the city, take a day, or two, or three, and see our countryside. A study in contrasts, all of it, and all of it much older than we are. If you miss it, you're missing half our local flavor—and a rare treat, to boot.

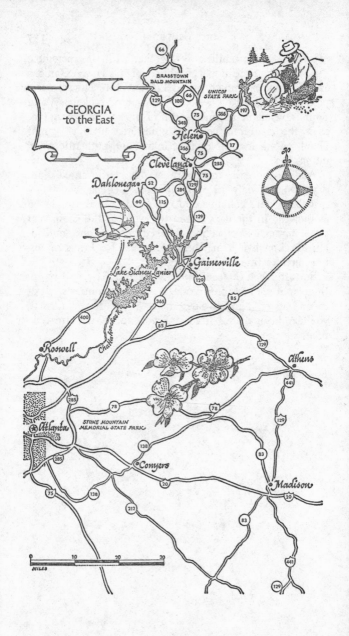

GEORGIA
-to the East

EAST

To the east of Atlanta, the hills soften and the air itself seems to become richer, gentler, somehow older. Here are the dreaming, small towns that were, in the days before the Civil War, the fountainheads of culture, polish, elegance, mannerly decorum. This region is probably richer in ante-bellum tradition and heritage than any in Georgia. A great many of the fine old Greek Revival residences, academies, churches, and civic buildings still stand; many are occupied today by descendants of their original builders, and it's not hard to imagine, on a still, spellbound summer twilight or a quiet, crystal winter evening, that the next moment will bring a faint ruffle of music and laughter, a whiff of lavender and rose water, a flash of crinoline and dimity. The past lingers longer and stronger in our East, and though these tours take you, in part, along Sherman's route to the sea, it's easy to understand why he simply could not bring himself to destroy some of these small towns. The general was not immune to the charm of a Georgia that once was. And neither will you be.

COLUMNS AND CLOISTERS
(7 to 9 hours—about 50 miles)

Today, you'll have a leisurely look at one of the loveliest little towns in the entire state: Madison. Long before the Civil War, this was a community of prosperous and cultivated cotton planters and merchants, who built their elegant homes and tended their blazing gardens and green lawns largely in the part of the town that's now called "Old Town." Legend has it that it was General Sherman who spared Madison from the overenthusiastic torch, but it was actually General Slocum, commander of Sherman's left wing. As the Union Army approached, one of the town's leading citizens, Senator Benjamin Hill, rode out to meet the troops and plead for the sparing of Madison. As

Hill had voted against secession and claimed friendship with Sherman, Slocum apparently decided that discretion was the better part of valor and spared the torch.

So most of Madison exists virtually untouched, as it did both before and after the war that set brother against brother. And a lovelier small town you never saw.

After a look at Madison, you'll come home by way of the tranquil and beautiful Monastery of the Holy Ghost, in Conyers, Georgia, with its great cloister, built entirely by the labor of the Trappist brothers who live and work there, its fine gardens, greenhouses, and lovely grounds.

To Madison: I-20 East, about 50 miles, exit Madison, right to center of town.

Your first stop in Madison should be the Madison-Morgan Cultural Center, on South Main Street. You'll find a brochure with a guide to the historic buildings in the city, plus a fine mapped bicycle tour of the city and the surrounding countryside. Bicycles can be rented at Bike World, on South Main Street. Call ahead to reserve one, at 342-3586. We can't recommend a more pleasant ride—gentle countryside, very little traffic, and some of the most beautiful and well-preserved ante-bellum architecture in the South. You can drive the routes too, and both driving and biking tour-guide booklets can be had from the police station as well as the Cultural Center.

Do take a spin around the square, with its handsome, ornate, brick storefronts, and then slip gently into Old Town. It's as close to the living ambience of the nineteenth century as you're likely to find anywhere. Here, along Academy Street and Old Post Road, you'll see Senator Hill's grand old home, as well as a host of other pre-Civil War residences and public buildings. Fine architecture lines other little streets and byways too. You can't get lost in Madison, but you can lose your heart. Well-tended gardens, great arching old trees, fountains splashing and birds singing—much of Madison seems simply unreal. You'll find some of the handsomest houses along Washington Street and Dixie Avenue. Also notable are

the Presbyterian Church on South Main Street, built in
the early 1800s, with Tiffany windows and a silver com-
munion service, which was stolen during the war and later
recovered; and magnificent Casulon Plantation (seven
miles from the town of Madison), the manor house of an
old ten-thousand-acre plantation featuring splendid box-
wood gardens. The manor and sixteen acres of ground are
open by appointment. Check by telephone. It is open several times a year for special occasions. Call the Cultural
Center for dates.

Madison, as might be expected, abounds with good,
small antique shops; you'll want to stop and poke around.
An especially nice one is Madison Colonial, next to the
courthouse. If it's getting toward lunchtime, you might
want to drop in at Ye Old Colonial Restaurant, on the
town square. Or bring a picnic lunch and enjoy it on the
grounds of Hill Park, just before you reach the Cultural
Center.

*To Conyers and the monastery: I-20 West, exit Con-
yers, L Rte. 138, R at fork, L South Cott Hwy., L into
monastery.*

The Monastery of the Holy Ghost was built entirely by
the labor and love of the Trappist brothers who inhabit it.
Most of the soaring Gothic cloister is closed to women,
but men are welcome to enter and reflect. Women may
visit the chapel, built totally by hand.

The greenhouse complex, where intricate displays of
cacti and bonsai are featured; the gift shop, which offers
lovely pottery and artifacts made by the brothers, and
wonderful bread, milled and baked on the premises; and
the spectacular grounds are open to everyone. An interesting slide presentation shows women the interiors of the
cloister and the daily life of the community. And if you've
packed a lunch, the tranquil green grounds are a soothing
and soul-restoring place to picnic.

*To Atlanta: leave monastery, R South Cott Hwy., R
Hwy. 138, L I-20 West to Atlanta.*

Also west of Madison on I-20 is Hard Labor Creek

State Park, with an 18-hole golf course, white sand beach, lakes for swimming and fishing, cabins, and picnic areas.

Exit I-20 at Rutledge and follow signs. Or if you are energetic, you may want to bicycle there from Madison, about twelve miles.

NORTH

It's been said that the Appalachian Mountains are the oldest mountains on earth—not raw and bristling with rock and tearing at the sky, as do the newer, upstart mountains of the world, but age-bearded, weather-gentled, softened into woman curves by the oppressive weight of oceans and aeons of time. Georgia's Blue Ridge Mountains are a part of the ancient Appalachians, and they wear their peculiar, luminous blue mist of age and air and aloneness like shawls on proud old women. This is some of the loveliest and most defiant land under the sun, hospitable to the outlander but never completely tamed. It's a country of musical place names and lingering myths passed on from the red men who walked it first, down to the proud, tough Scots who settled these hills after the Battle of Culloden. It's said that there's not a little Stuart blood in the Georgia mountains still, and, indeed, the hidden coves and valleys and the settlements beside the fast-running white rivers would have made fine homes for the wild, lonely Highlanders who fled their glens and mountains so precipitously.

Wherever they came from, the people of the Georgia mountains will make you at home in their beautiful country. Fairs, festivals, celebrations, and fetes abound. Whole villages are devoted to preserving the arts, crafts, and ambience of the hills. You'll see vast lakes, soaring waterfalls, dizzying gorges, a complete gold-rush village, state parks with wonderful outdoor things to do, Indian mounds and artifacts dating back to A.D. 1000, an entire resort world built on a series of islands in a vast blue lake, and more little shops offering arts, crafts, and antiques than you thought there were in the world. And you'll get a chance to sample some of the best mountain cooking under the sun. Lift up your eyes and follow your heart. You won't forget North Georgia.

THE HILLS ARE ALIVE
(8 to 9 hours or overnight)

This tour takes you from the city limits to the highest peak in Georgia and back again. Along the way, you can wander through a small Alpine village so authentically fitted out that it might have come straight from Bavaria; look things over from atop Brasstown Bald, where, on a clear day, you really can see forever (well, almost); stretch your muscles and spirit in a state-park area of incredible natural beauty and myriad recreational activities; marvel at a dizzying mountain waterfall in the Chattahoochee National Forest; and browse and buy in some of the most fascinating mountain arts-and-crafts shops this side of Switzerland. The places mentioned here are highlights; if you're doing a leisurely tour and plan to stop overnight somewhere, you'll find countless serendipitous spots on your own.

This tour is especially magnificent in the fall, through October, when the mountain frost has turned everything to blazing yellow, red, and bronze. But it's peaceful and lovely anytime.

From Atlanta: I-85 North, L on 365 Gainesville, exit Rte. 129, L Rte. 129 to Cleveland, L around square, R Rte. 75 at traffic light, straight to Helen.

Helen, Georgia, is a charming little fancy of a place that began life as a sawmill village in the early 1900s and has recently been completely transformed into as Bavarian a village as you're likely to find outside the real thing. Cobblestones, gingerbread, bright paint, window boxes, and squares rioting with flowers—Helen has it all. Here, too, you'll find a wonderful collection of Old World shops and cafés that will sell you just about anything you ever wanted or thought you did, with the accent on both imported and local mountain wares. There are cheese, candy, and bakery shops; tearooms and restaurants; and something special going in every season of the year, from square dancing to sports, to winter activities, to the colorful Oktoberfest, a lively celebration modeled around the real thing in Munich. Good all year, with summer theatre, Christmas celebrations, fall festivals, fishing and water sports, stables and fine golf, all in a truly lovely setting. Do take time to wander around the whole village. It doesn't take long.

From Helen, continue on Rte. 75 north, L Rte. 356, R Rte. 348 (Richard Russell Scenic Highway).

The Richard Russell Scenic Highway, designated Ga. 348, winds more than fourteen miles through some of the most beautiful mountain areas in the entire Southeast. If you have a camera, prepare to use it now. At the highway's highest point, Tessnatee Gap, you'll see the marker where the famed Appalachian Trail crosses the road. Drive slowly; this is truly spectacular country.

From Richard Russell Highway, R Rte. 180, follow signs to Brasstown Bald.

Brasstown Bald is the highest point in the state, soaring 4,784 feet above sea level. Known affectionately, if somewhat inaccurately, as "Little Switzerland," it truly is a wonder to behold. Four states and the whole misted panorama of the Blue Ridge Mountains are visible on a good day, and there's a fine, ultramodern visitors' center that has fascinating exhibits depicting the influence of man on this old earth since the days of the earliest Indians. There's an entrance fee, and it's well worth it. Center is open May 1 through October 31.

From Brasstown Bald, L 180 (becomes 66), R Rte. 75, L 356 to Unicoi Recreational Experiment Station.

Unicoi State Park, situated on a forested slope above a 52-acre lake, is a paradise for sportsmen and families. It has cottages, tent and trailer camping, swimming and picnic facilities, and a wonderful program of planned activities with emphasis on arts and crafts and nature and environmental studies. During the summers, especially, there's something going on all day every day, from folk singing to quilting and pottery demonstrations to canoeing, nature walks, and lectures and demonstrations at the lodge and amphitheater. Craft shop and general store, too.

Just a mile and a half north of Unicoi State Park is the lovely Anna Ruby Falls area, with fishing, hiking, and picnic facilities in the vast Chattahoochee National Forest, plus one of the most spectacular mountain waterfalls you ever saw. Bring out the cameras.

From Unicoi, continue 356 east, R 197, bear left at fork to continue on 197 to Mark of the Potter, about 3 miles.

Mark of the Potter is a totally enchanting craft shop converted from a corn mill on the Saque River. The emphasis is strongly on the beautiful pottery thrown from the shop's own special clay, and you can watch the whole process, from throwing to glazing to firing. There are also good contemporary handmade crafts in wood, metal, and fabric, all done by southeastern craftsmen—but it's the pottery that will fascinate you. Do take time to wander out on the porch over the old mill pond, where fat mountain trout disport themselves all year long.

You'll find a host of really interesting arts, crafts, and antique shops along the route. Most are directly on the roads, so you've only to stop wherever your fancy dictates and browse. There is some frankly tacky stuff here and there, but not much. These are, in the main, honest and authentic shops. For one of the most interesting, continue.

From Mark of the Potter, R Rte. 197 to sharp L Rte. 255.

Tekakwitha is an Indian and western crafts shop and museum that's sure to intrigue you and send your kids out of their minds. Named (so the story goes) after Kateri Tekakwitha, the "Lily of the Mohawks," the shop is crammed with a dizzying array of pottery, jewelry, sand paintings, baskets, clothing, tableware, western boots and accessories, wood carvings, and other Indian and western memorabilia. The shop wares are contemporary but authentic, and the museum areas are especially comprehensive and good. Do stop—but be prepared to part with some wampum, especially if you have youngsters along. (Did you ever go to the mountains without at least buying a pair of moccasins?)

Continue on Rte. 255 to Old Sautee Store.

The Old Sautee Store is a really fascinating, jumbled, and eccentric collection of store merchandise from the nineteenth and early-twentieth centuries. Much of it is real museum quality, and indeed, the store is, in part, a museum, but there's a good modern import shop, too. A trivia buff's paradise.

From the Old Sautee Store, follow Rte. 17 to L Rte. 75 to Cleveland, to Rte. 129 to Gainesville, R 365 to I-85, and return to Atlanta.

If you'd like to stay overnight along the way, the Unicoi Lodge, cottages, and campsites in Unicoi State Park are a natural. And there are good motels in and around Helen. The Helendorf Inn, overlooking the Chattahoochee River and featuring Bavarian décor, kitchens, and private balconies, is especially good. It's apt to be crowded, so write or call the Inn at P. O. Box 86, Helen, Georgia 30545. (404) 878-2271.

THERE'S GOLD IN THEM THAR HILLS
(8 to 9 hours or overnight)

This tour takes you far back into history, to the site of one of the country's first authentic gold rushes, where almost an entire town is devoted to preserving and celebrating the wild and wonderful boom-town days. Then you'll get a look at a whole village gone staunchly Bavarian and a chance to rest and invite your soul, as Thoreau said, in one of the Southeast's most beautiful state parks, high in the mountains. There are some superb shopping, antiquing, and arts-and-craftsing along the way, too. This is a comfortable day, or you can stay overnight and stretch it into two—or even a week. Unicoi State Park and Helen, Georgia, both have good accommodations.

North on I-85, L Gainesville Rte. 365, exit #6, Rte. 129 about 40 miles, L Rte. 129, continue 129 and

*Rte. 60, L on Rte. 60, follow 60 about 20 miles to
Dahlonega. Gold Hills on left.*

Dahlonega, Georgia, is quite simply a phenomenon. It
started life as a town around 1828, when a wandering
hunter overturned a rock and found it literally laced with
gold—and the rush was on. But gold had been here for
aeons before there was a town. The word "Dahlonega" is
the white man's version of the Indian name for the region,
"Ta lo ne ga," which, literally translated, means "Place of
Yellow Money." Millions of dollars' worth of gold was
mined from 1828 to the early 1900s—so much that the
federal government established a mint in Dahlonega in
1834.

But with the discovery of gold in California, Dahlonega
lost out in the rush, and the great mines slid into obscurity. There's still gold in the red hills around the city, and
the Crisson Mine, last worked in 1903, recently reopened
for small-scale operations and is open daily for visitors. The
Gold Hills of Dahlonega is simply not to be missed; we
suggest you spend a minimum of two hours here so you
can do and see everything there is in this city that gold
built.

Gold Hills, the re-created gold-mining city, features authentic mining equipment, restored buildings, tours, rides,
demonstrations, and best of all, the chance to pan for gold
yourself. Gold Hills and the Crisson Mine furnish pans,
gold-bearing soil, water, and free lessons—and you may get
a small nugget or two. But you will almost certainly see
gold specks among the dust.

In addition, there are guided tours of the old mines,
a fascinating old stamp mill, nature trails with interpretive stations to tell you the history of the gold era, and
a craft factory complete with demonstrations. Then there
are a wooden-toy factory, a crafts shop, a picnic pavilion
where you can eat your own lunch or one prepared by Gold
Hills, a museum of gold-mining equipment, and even a
few authentic moonshine stills. If you're lucky enough to
be in the area in late October, the three-day festival, Gold

Rush Days, is a giddy carnival of parades, square dances, mule and wagon races, and arts and crafts demonstrations. Wild! Gold Hills is open weekends only in April and May, and daily in June through October.

From Gold Hills, L on Rte. 60, less than a mile to the Smith House.

If you didn't have a picnic at Gold Hills, you must not miss the Smith House. This nationally famous old lodge has some of the best family-style eating you ever tasted, around wooden tables literally heaped with bowls and platters of fried chicken, meats, southern vegetables, fresh rolls—the works. There's a motel with swimming pool on the premises, too.

From the Smith House, continue on the same road to Dahlonega Square.

This pretty little square is an authentic re-creation of the one that served the brawling settlement in the gold-rush era, and you can have a wonderful time strolling along landscaped, tree-shaded pedestrian malls, poking into the fascinating little shops, or just sitting in the shade of an ancient sycamore tree. You'll certainly want to look through the gold museum on the square. It's the city's major attraction and is said to be the most visited historical site in the state. A diorama of a gold mine shows how it's done. And there are countless artifacts from the free-wheeling gold-rush days. The building was once the old Lumpkin County Courthouse and is the oldest building in North Georgia. It's open every day except Sunday morning and Monday. Free of charge.

Continue around the square to Rte. 60, R at fork about a mile and follow Rte. 52E to L Rte. 115, to Cleveland, Georgia. L around square, R Rte. 75 at light, follow 75 to Helen.

Pretty, old-world little Helen is a complete Alpine village that looks as though it were lifted out of a cranny of Bavaria and set down in North Georgia. Among the cobblestones, flower boxes, gingerbread, and gay paint you'll find a heady assortment of little shops offering just about anything under the mountain sun, with imported and local mountain wares a specialty. Then there are cafés; restaurants; cheese, candy, and bakery shops; ice cream parlors. If you didn't gorge at the Smith House, do stop here for a late lunch. Something is popping in Helen all year long, be it a square dance, summer theatre, Christmas celebration, fine fishing and water sports, horseback riding, golf, or the fabled Oktoberfest, modeled on the biggie in Munich. By all means, see the entire village. It's a wonderful little conceit.

From Helen, R Rte. 326 to Unicoi State Park.

Unicoi State Park makes a serene and spectacular respite from the bawdy bustle of the gold-rush era and the Bavarian fantasy of Helen. This park soars above a huge blue lake and offers fine cottages, tent and trailer camping, swimming and picnic facilities, and a wonderful program of planned activities ranging from folk singing to environmental studies, sports, crafts demonstrations, and nature walks. There are a lodge and amphitheater, too, as well as a craft shop and general store. Things are liveliest in the summer, but it's pretty any time.

While you're in Unicoi, do follow the signs to Anna Ruby Falls. Here are more fishing, hiking, and picnic facilities, and the picturesque waterfall plunging down the mountain gorge is color-film stuff.

While you're in the area, we heartily recommend you stop at Unicoi Station (signs will get you there) and pick up their fine little map of local points of interest in the general vicinity. It lists, among other things, most of the good little craft and antique shops that literally dot the area like freckles on a towhead's nose. There are many, and you'll find them all fun. One that's not to be missed is the Old Sautee Store.

If you're not pushed for time, this is a charmer. It's an eccentric and authentic jumble of old general-store merchandise garnered from the nineteenth and early-twentieth centuries, and there's a fine little museum section, too. If old-fashioned rural memorabilia isn't your bag, you'll probably find something in the modern import shop that is.

From the Old Sautee Store, return on Rte. 17 to L Rte. 75 to Cleveland, about 32 miles from Unicoi, to 129 to Gainesville. Then, R on 365 to I-85 to Atlanta.

FROM THE RED MAN'S VALLEY TO RED TOP MOUNTAIN
(7 to 8 hours or overnight)

This tour takes you to the Etowah Indian Mounds, near Cartersville, Georgia, one of the most significant and spectacular Indian archaeological sites in the Southeast, and to Red Top Mountain, a state park in the gentle foothills of the Blue Ridge Mountains, where there's a whole green world of wonderful outdoor things to do. It can be driven easily in four or five hours, but you may want to stay longer if you choose to linger at the mounds or in the park. We hope you will. Both are among the state's most outstanding attractions.

From Atlanta, N on I-75 to Rte. 41 to Cartersville to temporary end of 41 or Cartersville exit, about 30 miles. From Rte. 41, L at Etowah Indian Mounds sign. Follow Main Street (Rte. 61-293) 1.2 miles, sharp L at Etowah Street. Follow Etowah Mounds signs, 2.7 miles.

Nobody knows for sure if they were early Cherokees, Creeks, or an even earlier tribe, but the Indians who settled the peaceful village in the Etowah River Valley and built the imposing ceremonial mounds lived here from A.D. 1000 to 1500. What they left behind has been a priceless legacy to archaeologists all over the country and to the state of Georgia.

Etowah was the most important Indian settlement in the Etowah Valley and was the center of the political and religious life of the area. It was the home of chiefs who directed the growing, storage, and distribution of food, and was also the center where the red men of the valley gathered for their great religious festivals.

The town was fortified, surrounded on three sides by a

wood-post stockade and a moat, and on the fourth by the Etowah River. Using baskets for carrying, the Indians constructed a series of great pyramids, or mounds, from the rich earth near the moat. Chiefs lived atop the mounds, in elaborately decorated temples and residences, and elaborate burial rituals took place at the base of the mounds and in the funeral temples on their summit. The dead were buried in spectacular costumes, accompanied by special paraphernalia. When archaeological exploration was begun, initiated by the Smithsonian Institution in 1883, these great mounds began to give up astonishing and priceless treasures. Explorations have continued off and on through the years and have yielded, besides the skeletons and effigies of the Indians, a great many artifacts, both ceremonial and utilitarian, that can still be seen today.

Here are pottery artifacts of every description: wooden masks, ornaments and rattles, decorative wares, baskets, sewing and weaving tools, agricultural and hunting tools, even equipment from the ritual sports played in the village plaza.

At Etowah, you can walk the well-defined ruins of the village and see the remains of the major mounds. It's an eerie and fascinating journey back into man's earliest history. And by all means, see the fine interpretive museum, developed by the Georgia Historical Commission, which has a really excellent collection of the artifacts garnered over the years from the digs. The museum not only exhibits these priceless relics, it does a fine job of delineating the proud, gentle society that lived in this village on the Etowah. The entire area, including the museum, is open daily, and there's a small entrance fee.

Follow the same route back to Rte. 41.

Just a block on your right before you reach Rte. 41, you might want to stop and visit Southaire Antiques, a graceful ante-bellum house crammed with good American antiques. The great magnolias on the velvety lawn are a Cartersville landmark. Cartersville is also the home of the giant Philadelphia Carpet Company mill, and though our real carpet country is to the north, at Dalton, this is a fascinating stop if they have someone who might take you through. Call them at 382-5200 to see if there's a tour. We also suggest that if you haven't packed a lunch, you stop at one of the quick-food places in Cartersville on Rte. 41 and take it with you to Red Top. The park makes a lovely picnic spot, and while there's a snack bar open there in the summer, it's apt to be crowded.

From Main St., R Rte. 41, L to Red Top Mountain, about 3 miles. Watch for signs.

Lovely Red Top Mountain State Park, on the high hills around deep-blue Allatoona Lake, is a wonderful place for family unwinding. The area was a battleground during the Civil War, scene of fierce fighting from May to November 1864. But, today, it's all peace, laughter, and activity, and you'll want to sample some or all of it. Like all state parks, many of the recreational attractions are open all year long.

We suggest you take your lunch to the pretty picnic area overlooking the lake, with picnic tables, grills, and shelters. Then, if it's summer, you might take a swim at the white sand beach, where there's a combination bathhouse/snack bar open during the season. Swimming is allowed when there's a lifeguard on duty, which means all day in the summer. There's a small fee.

If you'd like to explore the vast blue lake, you can rent boats and motors at the nearby marina. There are a launching ramp and a gas dock close at hand. There are also docks in the mobile-home area.

Fishing is always good at Allatoona, and you can drop a line from the banks any time from 7:00 A.M. to 10:00 P.M. Any fisherman over sixteen must have a current state fishing license; the trading post will sell you one. They're not costly.

The trading post is where you check in if you're a camper. It sells all the usual concession items, plus groceries and sundries for campers. And, of course, the fishing licenses.

A miniature golf course near the beach can be a spritely diversion for the whole family. There's a small fee.

If you'd like to stay over at Red Top, rental cottages and mobile homes are modern, pretty, and inexpensive. All are fully set up for housekeeping, with stove and refrigerator, cooking and serving facilities, and linens. There's central heat in all, as well as air conditioning. The cottages have fireplaces, too. You'll need reservations; make them through the resident park superintendent at 974-5182. It's a local call from Atlanta.

And if you have a camper, there are several really lovely family camping areas with a total of one hundred and fifty sites. About fifty of them have water and electricity adjacent to the site. There are comfort stations with hot showers and laundry facilities, tables, and grills throughout the area, too. And a separate area accommodates large, self-contained campers. These have electricity and water at the sites, and dump-station facilities. There's a small overnight fee, and no reservations are necessary for any of the campsites.

To Atlanta: return to Rte. 41, then follow I-75 South; or when I-75 is complete, follow directly to Atlanta.

A note: Since the Etowah Indian Mounds are not open on Sunday mornings, you might want to reverse this tour. Just go on to Red Top first and come back by the mounds.

WATER, WATER EVERYWHERE
(6 to 8 hours or a weekend)

Lake Lanier Islands is an incredible water world lying in the shadow of the Blue Ridge Mountains, less than an hour's drive from Atlanta. It comes close to being all things to all people. You can drive up for a sail or a swim or a picnic, spend a leisurely day just exploring the entire 1,200 acres of islands, forest, and flowers, or stay a weekend or a week and do virtually everything there is to do under the sun. It's a particular favorite for Atlantans wanting a lose-the-world weekend just an hour away from home, and its mild climate lets visitors enjoy most of the facilities all year long. We suggest that if you've had a full week of exploring Atlanta and its environs, this is a wonderful weekend unwinder. Plan to stay over and let the lake and the mountains soothe away your troubles—or just run up for a bit. But do see it. The gates are open twenty-four hours a day, and there's a well-worth-it charge of $2.00 per car daily. Once you're inside, here's a sample of what's waiting for you:

Water things. There's a fine white sand beach for swimming, complete with diving docks, rafts, lounges, and lifeguards on duty in season. A sparkling bathhouse with showers and restrooms is right at hand. It's open weekdays and Sundays from 9:00 A.M. to 7:00 P.M., and Saturdays from 9:00 A.M. to 8:00 P.M. Beach and bathhouse facilities are free. There's a beach restaurant on the scene, too, with short orders during the day and a full menu at night.

From the beach, you can rent a fishing boat, a canoe, a kayak, a paddle boat, a catamaran, or a frisky little day sailer, anytime during beach hours. And in the summer season, there are free water shows staged six days a week by the islands' own crack ski team, the Aquastars. It has everything: pretty girls, kite and jump acts, clowns—the works.

You can also rent a motorized fishing boat or a lively little pontoon boat, any day you choose, from the docks at the aquatic center.

And for as much fun as is legal or moral, try a houseboat. These floating pleasure domes are fully equipped and ready to go, and there are miles of beautiful, isolated lake shore to discover on your own. You don't have to be an expert for these. Just lay in a supply of food and ice and go. For a day or a weekend, they can't be beat. These are located at the aquatic center, and you'll need a reservation. Call (404) 945-6731.

If you've got your own boat in tow, you can put in at the public docks at the aquatic center any day, where they'll also sell you fuel oil, ice, and soft drinks. A free public boat-launching ramp and trailer facility on South Sylvan Island is open daily.

Picnics. You can spread a feast any day during picnic season on North and South Sylvan islands, where there are more than two hundred family sites set in deep, cool woods overlooking the ever-present lake. There are charcoal grills, three group pavilions available by reservation, and a mini-restaurant that offers good short-order picnic fare in case you don't want to go the peanut-butter-and-jelly route. In the heart of the picnic area, a unique and beautiful children's playground is open daily, and there's competent supervision at posted times. Playground and picnic sites are free of charge.

Golf. It's glorious at Lake Lanier Islands. There's an 18-hole, par-72 championship course, complete with clubhouse, pro shop, lounge, and restaurants, that should challenge any player. It features six over-water holes, eight over-water shots, and 6,400 yards of sheer beauty. Stouffer's spectacular 256-room resort hotel, Pineisle, lies snuggled around the 18th hole. Better call for tee times at (404) 945-8955. Open every day, all year long.

There's also an 18-hole mini-golf course that's a hands-down family favorite. It features the same hazards and landscaping as its big-sister course and is lighted for night play. Clubs and balls are furnished. It opens every day at 11:00 A.M.

Riding. J-Rad Stables offers trail rides, bridle paths, and a pony ring for the kids. It's a fine way to spend part of a day.

Fishing. Besides all of Lake Sidney Lanier, you can drop a line at Rainbow Run, consisting of three beautifully terraced woodland trout ponds. The trout are fat and glossy, the bait and tackle are free, and you can have your catch cleaned, wrapped, and iced at no extra charge. Open daily from 10:00 A.M. to 7:00 P.M. and on weekends from 10:00 A.M. to dark.

Accommodations. There are three ways to stay overnight at Lake Lanier Islands, all different, all with appeal of their own. Families like the islands' two-bedroom rustic cottages, set in wooded hills on one of the islands. There are more than fifty of them, and all have central air conditioning and heating, dishwashers, disposals, sun decks, and fireplaces. There's a fold-out bed in living rooms, and all you need to bring are your family and your food. The cottages should be reserved. Call (404) 945-8331.

The campgrounds at Lake Lanier Islands occupy their own wooded peninsula out into the vast blue lake and offer pull-through or back-in RV sites with water and electricity. There are tent sites, too. All come with charcoal grills, picnic tables, and unique beauty and quiet. There are also comfort stations with showers and laundry equipment convenient to all sites, and sewer sites and a dump station are available. Then there's a free boat-launching ramp, boat-trailer parking, a fishing pier, and a recreation hall. No reservations, but you might call (404) 945-6773 to see how crowded things are. Open all year.

Pineisle. For people who want to rough it elegantly, Stouffer's stunning resort hotel offers 256 rooms, a glossy restaurant, snack bar, lounge, and nightclub with frequent name entertainment. There are ballroom and penthouse suites, and a glorious pool overlooking the velvet green of the golf course and the blue lake and mountains. Very plush, indeed. Call (404) 945-8955 or 1-800-323-4455, toll free, for reservations.

Stores and restaurants. They include the luxe facilities at Pineisle; the beach restaurant, with breakfast, lunch, and dinner year 'round and short-order take-out service; the mini-restaurant, open during picnic season and offering hot dogs, hamburgers, sandwiches, ice cream, and cold drinks; the campers' store, at the campground entrance and offering fresh and canned food all year; and the village harbor store, with all manner of groceries and supplies, in the Mediterranean-style village harbor complex.

Other goodies. Well, there's free shuttle bus service to all parts of the islands, in season. And a fine welcome cen-

ter. And an authority and administration building to see
that things run smoothly. Guards at the gates. And medi-
cal and police assistance on call.

But, mainly, it's the beauty, serenity, proximity, and the
excellence of details and upkeep that lure Atlantans in
droves to Lake Lanier Islands. You really ought to sample
all of it.

*From I-285 or downtown Atlanta to I-85 North, L
365 to Gainesville, exit #2 Friendship Road, turn L
and follow signs to Lake Lanier Islands and Pineisle—
about 4 miles.*

SOUTH

To the south of the city, the hills smooth out gently and the fields and woods are lush, green, and soft. This is some of the best farming country in the world, and you'll see miles of orchards, vegetables, grain, and melons rioting unashamedly in season. History lingers almost unchanged here. Middle Georgia largely escaped the punishing fist of the Civil War, and in town after sleepy small town there are graceful, white-columned ante-bellum houses and dreaming old courthouse squares, not untouched, certainly, but seeming so to the casual eye. Everything is a bit slower to our south, a bit smoother, richer, older, softer. Flowers and fruit trees bloom earlier, and autumn's bonfire burns later and longer. This is some of the most beautiful country in the world, gentle for the most part, but broken down its spine by the defiant green mountains that mark the dying of the Appalachian chain.

To the south, you'll see Atlanta's roots, the languid and lovely old heritage of time, the land, the agriculture that lent its grace to the raw young city to the north. Here are historical sites and preservations, glorious things blooming all year long, and a look at Georgia as it might have been more than a century ago. Be warned: the dramatic contrast between Atlanta present and Georgia past is potent sorcery.

RUFFLES AND FLOURISHES
(*7 to 9 hours or overnight*)
On this tour, you'll see the poignant and much-visited Little White House, which President Franklin Roosevelt held so dear, and where he died. It's a treasure trove of the history and memorabilia of this dynamic man, and a fascinating insight into his basic simplicity and humanity, which charmed and comforted a troubled nation.

Then on to Callaway Gardens, an incredible 2,500-acre family resort and gardens complex, where some of the most spectacular flowers in the world bloom all year long in gardens and greenhouses, and where there's enough truly fine recreational activity to keep an entire family happy all year long.

And you'll finish up at Hamilton on the Square, a charming and complete 1840s town re-created with loving care and great authenticity, relatively new but already a premier attraction for Atlantans and visitors.

This is a comfortable day's drive, but if you should lose your heart and want to stay over (and we suspect you will) Callaway Gardens is the place for it. You couldn't use it up in a year, and it's one of the Southeast's most favored vacation spots. So consider making a weekend of it.

From Atlanta, I-85 South, exit Alternate 27 South, follow L fork to Warm Springs; at Warm Springs, take 85W south, R into the grounds of the Little White House.

Franklin Roosevelt first came to Warm Springs in 1924, to seek relief in its natural warm-water pools from the crippling bout of polio that struck him in 1921. He was so charmed with the Springs, the countryside, and the people that he selected a site and built the Little White House there. He was instrumental in developing the Georgia Warm Springs Foundation, so that others similarly afflicted might benefit from the place he held dear, but it was the simple, rustic Little White House that he loved perhaps best of all his residences, and he spent much time there until his death, on April 12, 1945.

Little has been changed at the Little White House since the day of his death. Mementos abound. His wheelchair, the ship models he cherished so, his beloved Fala's chain, books, photos, and other treasures. Visitors may wander through the house at will, looking into each room. There is a taped commentary as you walk through, but no formal guided tours.

Aside from the dining area, the President's bedroom, the sun deck he so loved, the living area, and two more bedrooms, you'll want to see the famous unfinished portrait, for which he was sitting when death struck him that April day; his 1938 Ford Convertible, specially fitted with hand controls, in which he delighted; the guesthouse, where heads of state from all over the world slept; the old Warm Springs stagecoach; the memorial fountain and the Walk of States, with stones and flags from many states, leading to the Franklin D. Roosevelt Museum.

This museum is especially fascinating for children. Somehow, seeing the very personal memorabilia of this man makes him vividly alive. There's also an excellent documentary sound movie in the museum, *A Warm Springs Memoir of Franklin D. Roosevelt*, available at no charge. (There is an entrance fee.) A snack bar and gift shop are in the entrance building.

It's hard to explain why visitors find the Little White House so uniquely moving. In part, perhaps, it's the near-haunted air that lingers about it, as if he had just been out for a ramble and might come smiling into the cottage at any moment. Whatever, it's a heady and touching experience, and should not be missed.

From Warm Springs, R 85W south, R 190 west, R Rte. 27 north to Callaway Gardens.

This drive takes you through beautiful Franklin Roosevelt State Park. As you drive along the ridge of the mountain, the scenery is breath-taking. The former President had many of the pine trees planted there. You'll want to stop at areas provided just to enjoy the serenity and to take pictures.

Callaway Gardens in any season is an enchantment to mind, body, and spirit. There's a wealth of recreation activity here, but if you're limited for time, concentrate on the gardens and come back to catch the sports later. The growing things are unparalleled in this part of the world.

Callaway Gardens has miles and miles of marked hiking and bicycle trails through various areas of natural beauty, as well as fine automobile roads. Built on the green hills around a complex of quiet lakes, Callaway winds and wanders through 2,500 wooded acres, and there's something glorious everywhere you look. If you're limited for time, there are guided bus tours, which hit the highlights of the Gardens, scheduled at regular intervals throughout the day, all year long. You should take one. There's no better way to get at least a taste of the scope here. Ask at the visitors' gate. (There's an entrance fee.)

There's something beautiful growing outside in all seasons, so it doesn't really matter when you visit. Spring sees acre after acre of azaleas, dogwood, flowering trees, and bulbs. Summer is a riot of daylilies, crepe myrtle, summer flowers. Fall is flagrantly spectacular with the blazing foliage of the hardwoods. And winter is the time for the vivid holly trails. The Gardens' world-famous greenhouses, of course, are open all year, with exotic and not-so plants and flowers displayed in all their glory all year long. The conservatory greenhouse exhibits chrysanthemums, poinsettias, daffodils, tulips, and begonias in season all year long. A special six-acre outdoor display area shows off seasonal blooms in all their massed splendor. All in all, the growing things of Callaway Gardens are a marvel unto themselves.

What else? Well, if you want to stay a while, you can swim at the longest man-made beach in the world, in season, in a special swimming lake. Or play golf on four challenging courses—three fine 18-holers and a snappy nine. Hike, ride horseback, take a nature walk, play tennis, fish, boat, hunt quail in season, shoot skeet and trap, visit the pioneer log cabin and old covered bridge, see the enchanting little English-Gothic Ida Cason Callaway Memorial Chapel, tucked away by a waterfall in a quiet wood, or take part in several luminous annual events. The thrilling Florida State "Flying High" Circus spends the summer at Callaway and performs daily under the big top on the beach. Performers also serve as counselors for the Gardens' unique summer recreation program, a family-oriented affair literally crammed with activities and events for the whole tribe. The Gardens' top-notch water-ski tournament is held here each season.

There's a fine program of winter activities, too. You might want to check into the excellent winter weekend vacation packages and the annual Christmas celebration.

You can stay in the fine, 365-room Holiday Inn or rent an air-conditioned, one-or-two-bedroom cottage in the woodlands. You can dine really sumptuously off mouth-watering southern cooking, both at the picturesque Gardens clubhouse and at the Plantation Room at the Holiday Inn. You might want to lunch at one of these if you're making a day of it. If you want more information about rentals and reservations, write or call Callaway Gardens, Pine Mountain, Georgia 31822. (800-663-2281)

From Callaway Gardens, S on Rte. 27 3 miles to Hamilton on the Square.

Hamilton on the Square, in Hamilton, Georgia, is an intriguing and authentic little ante-bellum village, re-created with a fine eye for authenticity, centered on the town square in Hamilton, Georgia. It's a unique experience. Here you can actually experience life as it was lived by Georgians circa 1840. You can watch artisans and craftsmen working, and buy their wares; see their architecture and artifacts both in museums and in use; dine the way they did; even carouse a bit—genteelly—the way they did. In Hamilton on the Square, you'll find fascinating stores, museums, and even a theatre and movie house showing wonderful old flicks of the Keystone Cops era. Some of the area's most elegant dining is available at Hamilton Hall, a splendidly restored Victorian mansion with excellent Continental dining and extremely fine wine list with vintages dating back to 1928. Open for dinner only. There's ample time to dine and get back to the city fairly early.

For return to Atlanta: 27 north to Rte. 18 east, bear R through Harris City, L at Alternate 27 north, I-85 North to Atlanta.

A Day in Carter Country
(*All day*)

For hundreds of years, the sleepy little town of Plains (population 683) has dreamed tranquilly in its sunny corner of southwestern Georgia, its quiet life punctuated by little more than the slow, graceful drama of the changing seasons and cycles of planting and harvesting. Now, thanks to a smiling, softly drawling phenomenon known as Jimmy Carter, it's on the map in a way its townspeople never dreamed possible. This day will take you south and a bit west, through some of Georgia's loveliest old towns and richest farmland, to Plains, Georgia, birthplace and home of the thirty-ninth President of the United States.

> *From downtown Atlanta: I-75 South past Hapeville exit, R on 41/19, R 19 South past Ellaville, R 153, L Highway 45 to Plains.*

Plains looks as though Norman Rockwell might have invented it. It would be a movie set for a film made in the South decades ago: old white frame houses, towering old trees, cotton and peanut fields stretching away to the horizon, townspeople whose grandparents and great-grandparents grew up here moving slowly and serenely on their rounds of shopping and errands, children and rangy dogs jostling on their way to school. Its special charm is that, though the Carter bandwagon has skyrocketed it into national prominence and visitors swarm through the quiet streets by the hundreds, it really hasn't changed much physically, and isn't likely to. Plains people like their town the way it is. Even their beloved Jimmy, in whom they take great, wondering pride, isn't going to change that. They're as near the world's idea of classic small-town Southerners as you'll find left in the world, and fine people to know.

Plains proper is easy to see. You don't need a map or directions to find the points of interest you've been reading about in the national newspapers and magazines. Everything's right there on the main street. Plains's business section, and many of its residences and civic structures, occupy one side of a street running through town and out again, westward toward the Georgia-Alabama border. Railroad tracks occupy the other side of the street. Park your car anywhere you can find a space downtown, and walk. It won't take long.

Perhaps the main and most colorful single structure in downtown Plains is the old converted railroad depot, which now serves as headquarters for the President and his staff when they're in town, and also as a base for the news media. This picturesque old building is akin to many, many old railroad depots throughout the South, and is a favorite haunt of Miss Lillian, the President's handsome, peppery mother, who is often to be found ensconced in a rocking chair on the premises, passing the time of day with visitors and signing an occasional autograph.

Also, close at hand is the modest wooden Plains Baptist Church, where the President attends services whenever he's at home and where he long taught Sunday-school classes and still does occasionally. The little schoolhouse is nearby, too, site of the famous Carter staff-press softball games during the President's 1976 campaign. Under the town water tower, you may still be able to see a few trailers left from "TV City," the hastily assembled quarters for the national television networks, dating from the frenzied days of the campaign. The Carter family's enormous peanut warehouse isn't far away. Someone will point it out to you, but it's best to inquire if you can walk through. It's a working business and may be off limits to casual viewers.

You'll want to stop off at Billy Carter's service station. Though there's little to see except the accouterments of a working small-town service station, the President's friendly, garrulous brother may be on hand dispensing his common-sense, down-home words of wisdom. He's a great crowd pleaser. And Hugh Carter, a cousin who has owned a general store for many years, has recently converted it to a gift and antique shop where you can find all manner of

Carter memorabilia, including almost anything in the shape of a peanut. It makes for fascinating browsing.

At this writing, the President's home is, of necessity, closed to the public, and the streets surrounding it barricaded. You can probably drive by the girlhood home of the First Lady, though. Ask anyone. There is a small tour of Plains available that takes you past the President's boyhood home and other points of interest. Check at the depot to see when it leaves. You can also see the nursing home where Miss Lillian worked when Jimmy was a boy. It's a first-rate establishment and owes much to her energy and interest. The home was once the Wise Hospital, and the President was born there. Fire destroyed the hospital many years ago, and the nursing home was built in its place. It's on the south side of town.

Food facilities are scarce in Plains, so you may want to consider stopping off in Americus on your way down or back. Quite a good restaurant has recently opened in Plains, but it's small, and you can't count on being accommodated. Or you might want to bring a picnic lunch and find a likely shady spot.

Don't go to Plains expecting pomp, circumstance, and sophisticated facilities for tourists; they aren't there. But for a glimpse of rural Georgia as it has been for many, many years, the *real* South, perhaps, this charming little village is perfect. Small southern towns like this are fast passing from the American scene, and when they're gone, a way of life that is unique will go with them. Go with a light heart, a relaxed and nostalgic frame of mind, and a leisurely day at your disposal, and Plains, Georgia, will steal your heart.

To return to Atlanta, east on 280 to Americus, North on 19, follow 19 back to I-75/I-85 North, follow into downtown.

Facts and Fables

Like all cities of any age and size, Atlanta has its favorite legends—rich, glinting stories with one foot in fact and one in legend. There are thousands of them, springing from our time-shrouded past, when the red men walked these hills; from our brawling, scrappy, happy-go-lucky pioneer railroad days; from the agony and human majesty surrounding the Civil War; from our very hills and trees and river valleys. Here are four, of varying degrees of accuracy, that you're most likely to hear:

Peachtree Street, as everybody knows, was so named because of the flowering peach trees that lined its shoulders in our pioneer days; right? Wrong, according to a cherished local legend. By all rights, it should have been called Pitch Tree Street. The story goes that before the first white settlers came into Georgia, the Cherokee and Creek Indians who lived in the forest that became Atlanta had a favorite giant pine tree, standing tall where modern-day Peachtree now runs. They came for miles to this tree for the fat "pitch," or pine resin, which was invaluable for starting fires, patching bows, and whatever. They called it the "standing pitch tree," and when the white men trickled into Georgia, they corrupted the term into "peachtree" and named the main artery of their new settlement after it. So much for peach blossoms.

The Creeks and the Cherokees, so it's been said, were once great friends and coexisted happily in these forests for generations. Historians tell us that Atlanta and its environs was Creek country, and the country to the north, well into North Carolina and Tennessee, was the domain of the Cherokees. Fancy has it that this division came about as the result of a friendly game of La Crosse or its equivalent between the Creek and Cherokee nations, held on the banks of the Chattahoochee River. The boys got to whooping it up, according to the story, and someone had the bright idea of using the game to divide the territory. As a result, the Creeks are said to have won the land south of the Chattahoochee, and the Cherokees the land north of it. This is absolutely unverifiable, but as good an explanation as any to Atlantans' minds.

The City of Trees is a term you'll often hear applied to Atlanta. And it's true. Atlanta is literally carved out of a forest, you've only to go up to one of the restaurants or lounges atop Atlanta's skyscrapers to see that the great surf of green laps even into downtown. In fact, the U. S. Forestry Service tells us that Atlanta is officially designated a city in a forest—the only major city in the United States, to their knowledge, to have that official classification. Not a momentous thing to know, but a nice one.

The Dogwood City is our own, unofficial name for our city. And if you're here during the early spring, you'll see why. Atlanta is literally drowned in a flood of pink and white lace. So the Legend of the Dogwood is particularly dear to Atlantans; it belongs to the world, of course, but we think of it as our own. It goes like this: The dogwood was the tree that was chosen to provide the timber for the cross of Christ, and this gentle tree was greatly distressed at being used for such a purpose. Jesus felt this from the cross and said to the dogwood, "You have shown pity and sorrow for my suffering, and because of this, I promise you that never again shall a dogwood tree grow large enough to be used for a cross to crucify. From now on, you will grow slender and gnarled, and your blossoms will form a cross, with two long and two short petals. At the outer edge of each petal will be nail prints, stained rust-brown and red for my blood, and in the center of your flower will be a crown of thorns. And all who look upon you will remember."

You can be "facted" to death about Atlanta. Good,

solid information about the city abounds in any number of excellent, easily accessible publications. We've tried not to burden you in this book with more hard, dry facts than you ever wanted to know. But you *will* want to know about the following:

The *weather* is much discussed in Atlanta, as it is anywhere else, and has a great deal of bearing on what you'll bring to wear and what you can do when. Atlanta *is* a Deep South city, but because of our unusually high elevation (1,051 feet above sea level), we're spared much of the humid heat that shrouds other cities of the Deep South. The climate is generally mild all year long; it *can* get brutally cold in the winter and stifling in the summer, but it's rare, indeed, that these spells last long. Spring and fall linger long here, and both are sheer delights. You can play outdoor sports all year long if you're hardy, and for about nine months out of the year in comfort. Don't expect to swim before late April or after September, though. Winter and early spring can be pretty rainy; a lightweight raincoat is a good idea in fall, winter, and spring, and can serve as a topcoat, too, unless it's dead winter. A folding umbrella never hurt anybody anytime. Summer and fall are usually dry.

Dress is flexible. Atlanta is an extremely cosmopolitan city, and there are no fixed rules of dress. Like New York, Chicago, San Francisco, and other large, cosmopolitan cities, you'll see anything being worn at any time, from Levi's and tee shirts downtown to long or short cocktail and dinner dresses at the better restaurants, the theatre, and such. You'll probably be happy and go comfortably— from our cosmopolitan downtown to our chic suburbs to our deep country—if you bring well-cut pant suits, simple, easy dresses, tailored slacks and sweaters and blouses, and maybe a suit or dress with a jacket. A short cocktail dress will take you anywhere in the evening, though Atlanta women traditionally favor long, not-so-dressy clothes for evenings out. An affair like the Metropolitan Opera or a ball can call for your glittering-est big guns, but you can go in a short dress even to these with impunity. We're in cottons and lightweights by April and wear them until mid-October, but our winters do call for wools and tweeds and winter-weight coats.

Men use their common sense in Atlanta. If they're the coat-and-tie type at home, Atlanta won't change them. You'll see denim and/or ruffles and flourishes in the city's fanciest spots, right along with the good blue suits and occasional dinner jackets. Well-tailored-and-cut anything goes anywhere. (Almost; you wouldn't wear Levi's and boots to the opera, would you?) There are few real snobs in Atlanta's better places. Nowadays, most major restaurants do not require ties, but if you're undecided, ask when you phone for reservations. Obviously, you'll be more comfortable in some of our elegant eateries in a tie than in Levi's. Lightweight suits are fine all year, but you'll be glad of seersucker and cotton in August.

The Creative Team

Author Anne Rivers Siddons grew up in Fairburn, Georgia, some twenty miles to the southwest of Atlanta, and has lived in the city proper for many years. She has worked as an advertising copywriter and gained her wide knowledge of Atlanta while she was senior editor for *Atlanta* magazine and a writer for *Georgia* magazine. Anne has had articles published in *House Beautiful* and is the author of two books, a non-fiction work entitled *John Chancellor Makes Me Cry*, published by Doubleday, and a novel, *Heartbreak Hotel*, published by Simon & Schuster. She and her husband live in Atlanta's Buckhead section.

Series creator and consultant for the Atlanta Guide, Marge McDonald is founder and former president of Tourgals, Inc., a sightseeing and convention-service company catering to groups visiting Atlanta. Marge now serves as president of Ga. Hospitality & Travel Assn. She has served on the Executive Board of Directors of the Atlanta Convention and Visitors Bureau for several years, and has been co-chairman of its Tourism Committee, and has also served as treasurer of the Bureau. She has been a member of the Board of Trustees of the Atlanta Council for International Visitors and a board member of the Georgia Travel Commission and has held offices in both these organizations. Marge and her husband reside in the suburbs of Atlanta with their three children.

Atlanta-area Hotel and Motel List

All listed hotels and motels in this book are recommended by the Georgia Hotel-Motel Association or by the Atlanta Convention and Visitors Bureau.

KEY TO SERVICES:

BS	Baby sitting
CL	Cocktail lounge
E	Entertainment
FS	Food service
FU	Family units
GR	Game room
GC	Golf course
GP	Golf privileges
HC	Health club
HP	Heated pool
JT	Jogging track
K	Kitchenettes
KF	Kennel facilities
PA	Pets allowed
PG	Playground
P	Pool
SB	Sauna baths
TC	Tennis courts

Fishing, boating, and riding are listed for properties that offer these.

HOTELS AND MOTELS IN THE ATLANTA AREA

Admiral Benbow Inn—190 rooms. 1470 Spring St., Atlanta (30309). Tel. 872-5821. FS, CL, E, P, BS, PA, GP.

Admiral Benbow Inn Airport—258 rooms. 1419 Virginia Ave., Atlanta (30340). Tel. 768-3625. FS, CL, E, P.

Air Host Inn—300 rooms. 1200 Virginia Ave., Atlanta (30320). Tel. 767-7451. FS, CL, HP, E, HC.

Atlanta American Motor Hotel—350 rooms. Spring St. at Carnegie Way, Atlanta (30301). Tel. 688-8600. FS, CL, E, P.

Atlanta Cabana Motor Hotel—200 rooms. 870 Peachtree St., NE, Atlanta (30383). Tel. 875-5511. FS, CL, E, P, PA.

Atlanta Central Travelodge—70 rooms. 31 Courtland St., NE, Atlanta (30303). Tel. 659-4545. FS, FU, HP.

Atlanta Hilton Hotel—1250 rooms. 255 Courtland St., NE, Atlanta (30303). Tel. 659-2000. FS, CL, E, P, HC, TC, PA, JT, TC.

Atlanta Internationale Hotel—525 rooms. 450 Capitol Ave., at the Stadium, Atlanta (30312). FS, CL, E, HP, PA.

Atlanta Peachtree Travelodge—59 rooms. 1641 Peachtree St., NE, Atlanta (30309). Tel. 873-5731. FU, P, HP, BS, PA.

Atlanta Townehouse Motor Inn—302 rooms. 100 Tenth St., NW, Atlanta (30309). Tel. 892-6800. FS, CL, P, BS.

Atlantan Hotel—265 rooms. Luckie at Cone sts., Atlanta (30303). Tel. 524-6461. FS, CL, FU, SB.

Center Inn, The—150 rooms. 231 Ivy St., NE, Atlanta (30303). Tel. 577-1510. FS, CL, E, P, PA.

Century Center Motor Hotel—300 rooms. 2200 Century Parkway, NE, Atlanta (30345). Tel. 325-0000. FS, CL, E, P.

Century Inn Airport—175 rooms. I-285 & Riverdale Rd., Atlanta (30349). Tel. 996-4321. FS, CL, E, FU, P.

Clairmont Emory Inn—120 rooms. 1706 Clairmont Rd., Decatur (30033). Tel. 634-3311. FS, CL, P, PG, PA.

Colony Square Hotel—500 rooms. Peachtree & Fourteenth sts., Atlanta (30361). Tel. 892-6000. FS, CL, E, P, BS.

Cox Carlton Hotel—138 rooms. 683 Peachtree St., NE, Atlanta (30308). Tel. 872-7721. PA.

Days Inn Atlanta, Clairmont Road—909 rooms. I-85 & Clairmont Rd., Atlanta (30329). Tel. 633-8411. FS, K, FU, P, PG, PA.

Days Inn Atlanta, Shallowford Road—150 rooms. I-85 & Shallowford Rd. Exit, Atlanta (30345). Tel. 633-8451. FS, P, PG, PA.

Days Lodge—67 suites. 2792 Shallowford Rd., Atlanta (30341). Tel. 458-8821. K, FU, P, PA.

Decatur Inn—34 rooms. 921 Church St., Decatur (30030). Tel. 378-3125. K, FU, P.

Dunfey's Royal Coach—400 rooms. 1750 Commerce Dr., NW, Atlanta (30318). Tel. 351-6100. FS, CL, E, P, PA, GR, TC.

Emory Pines Inn—32 rooms. 1650 Clifton Rd., NE, Atlanta (30329). Tel. 634-5152. K, FU, P.

Georgian Terrace Hotel—165 rooms. 658 Peachtree St., NE, Atlanta (30308). Tel. 872-6671. FS, CL, E, BS.

Helendorf Inn—66 rooms. Box 86, Helen (30545). Tel. 878-2271. FU, KF.

Hilton Inn, Airport—350 rooms. 1031 Virginia Ave., Atlanta (30354). Tel. 767-0281. FS, CL, E, P, PG, PA.

Holiday Inn Airport—500 rooms. 1380 Virginia Ave., Atlanta (30320); P. O. Box 20773. Tel. 762-8411. FS, CL, E, P, PG, BS, PA.

Holiday Inn Atlanta, I-75/Perimeter—166 rooms. I-75 South at I-285, Atlanta (30354). Tel. 766-7511. FS, P, PA.

Holiday Inn Downtown—473 rooms. 175 Piedmont Rd., NE, Atlanta (30303). Tel. 659-2727. FS, CL, E, P.

Holiday Inn I-20 East—167 rooms. 4300 Snapfinger Woods Dr., Atlanta (30304). Tel. 981-5670. FS, CL, E, P, GP, PG, KF.

Holiday Inn I-85/Monroe Drive—253 rooms. 1944 Piedmont Cir., Atlanta (30324). Tel. 875-3571. FS, CL, E, P, GP, BS, PA.

Holiday Inn Marietta—330 rooms. 2360 Delk Rd., Marietta (30060). Tel. 427-8161. FS, CL, E, P, PG, PA.

Holiday Inn, Northeast—199 rooms. 4422 N.E. Expressway, Atlanta (30340). Tel. 448-7220. FS, CL, E, P, PG, PA, KF.

Holiday Inn, Northwest—207 rooms. 1810 Howell Mill Rd., Atlanta (30325). Tel. 351-3831. FS, CL, E, P, PG, PA.

Holiday Inn Six Flags—229 rooms. 4225 Fulton Industrial Blvd., Atlanta (30336). Tel. 691-4100. FS, CL, E, PA, KF.

Holiday Inn South I-75/US 41—180 rooms. 6288 Old Dixie Hwy., Atlanta (30236). P, PG, PA, KF, BS.

Holiday Inn Callaway Gardens—365 rooms. U. S. Hwy. 27, Pine Mountain (31822). Tel. 663-2281. FS, HP, GC, TC, PG, BS, KF. Also beach area, water skiing, fishing, quail shooting.

Hospitality Motor Inn—200 rooms. I-285 & Camp Creek Parkway, East Point (30344). Tel. 762-5141. FS, CL, E, HP, BS, TC, PG.

Howard Johnson's Motor Lodge—83 rooms. 5793 Roswell Rd., NW, Atlanta (30342). Tel. 252-6400. FS, P, PA.

Howard Johnson's Motor Lodge, Airport—200 rooms. 1377 Virginia Ave., Atlanta (30344). Tel. 762-5111. FS, CL, E, P, PA.

Howard Johnson's Motor Lodge, Northeast—160 rooms. 2090 N. Druid Hills Rd., NE, Atlanta (30329). Tel. 636-8631. FS, CL, P, PG, BS, PA.

Howard Johnson's Motor Lodge, Northwest—106 rooms. 1701 Northside Dr., NW, Atlanta (30318). Tel. 351-6500. FS, P, PG, BS, PA, KF.

Howard Johnson's Motor Lodge, South—215 rooms. 759 Washington St., SW, Atlanta (30315). Tel. 688-8665. FS, HP, SB, PG, PA, KF.

Howell House Hotel—161 rooms. 710 Peachtree St., NE, Atlanta (30308). Tel. 881-9999. FS, CL, K, FU.

Hyatt Regency Atlanta—1000 rooms. 265 Peachtree St., NE, Atlanta (30303). Tel. 577-1234. FS, CL, E, HP.

Intown Motor Hotel—73 rooms. 89 Luckie St., NW, Atlanta (30303). Tel. 524-7991. FS, CL, E, FU, P.

Journey's End Inn—156 rooms. I-75 Lockheed-Dobbins AFB Exit, Marietta (30067). Tel. 428-9451. FS, CL, E, P.

Landmark Inn—210 rooms. 1152 Spring, at Fourteenth St., Atlanta (30309). Tel. 873-4361. FS, CL, E, FU, P.

Mark Inn Southwest, Best Western—50 rooms. I-285 at Old National Hwy. Exit, Atlanta (30349). Tel. 768-0040. FS, CL, E, P, PA.

Marriott Motor Hotel—800 rooms. Courtland St. & International Blvd., Atlanta (30303). Tel. 659-6500. FS, CL, E, HP, BS, GR, HC, SB.

Marriott Motor Hotel at Perimeter Center—307 rooms. 246 Perimeter Center Pkwy., NW, Atlanta (30346). Tel. 393-6500. FS, CL, E, HP, S, GP, TC, GR.

Master Hosts Inn, East—100 rooms. I-20 at Wesley Chapel Rd., Decatur (30305). Tel. 288-6911. FS, CL, P, PA.

Master Hosts Inn, Northwest—101 rooms. I-75 at Lockheed Dobbins Exit, Marietta (30060). Tel. 427-8141. FS, CL, E, P, PA.

Master Hosts Inn, Southwest—100 rooms. I-85 & I-285 at Old National Hwy., College Park (30349). Tel. 768-5500. FS, CL, P, PA.

Northlake Hilton Inn—200 rooms. 4156 LaVista Rd., Tucker (30084). Tel. 938-1026. FS, CL, E, P, KF.

Old South Motel—101 rooms. 331 Cleveland Ave., SW,
    Atlanta (30315). Tel. 767-7441. FS, CL, FU, P, BS,
    PA.

Olde English Inn—120 rooms. 1900 Glenfair Rd., Decatur
    (30035). Tel. 288-7550. FS, CL, E, PA.

Omni International Hotel/Atlanta—500 rooms. One
    Omni International, Atlanta (30303). Tel. 659-0000.
    FS, CL, E, BS.

Pascal's Motor Hotel—120 rooms. 830 Martin Luther
    King Dr., SW, Atlanta (30314). Tel. 577-3150. FS,
    CL, E, P.

Peachtree Center Plaza Hotel—1081 rooms. 229 Peachtree
    St., NE, Atlanta (30303). Tel. 659-1400. FS, CL, E,
    P, HC.

Quality Inn, Marietta—47 rooms. 637 Cobb Parkway,
    Marietta (30062). Tel. 427-7272. FS, FU, P, BS, PA.

Radisson Olympic Inn—400 rooms. I-285 & Chamblee-
    Dunwoody Rd., Atlanta (30341). Tel. 394-5000. FS,
    CL, E, HP, HC, TC, BS.

Ramada Inn, Airport—180 rooms. 845 N. Central Ave.,
    Atlanta (30355). Tel. 763-3551. FS, CL, E, P.

Ramada Inn Central—450 rooms. I-85 & Monroe Drive,
    Atlanta (30324). Tel. 873-4661. FS, CL, E, P, PA.

Ramada Inn, Marietta—153 rooms. 2255 Delk Rd.,
    Marietta (30060). Tel. 422-7581. FS, CL, P.

Ramada Inn, Six Flags—154 rooms. 305 Industrial Circle,
    just off I-20 West, Atlanta (30336). Tel. 691-9390.
    FS, CL, E, P, PG, BS, PA.

Red Carpet Inn, Northeast—148 rooms. I-85 at Chamblee-
    Tucker Rd., Atlanta (30341). Tel. 451-9125. FS,
    CL, E, P, PA.

Red Carpet Inn, South—170 rooms. I-75 South of I-285,
    Atlanta (30350). Tel. 363-1100. FS, P, PA, PG.

Riviera Hyatt House—314 rooms. 1630 Peachtree St.,
    NW, Atlanta (30304). Tel. 875-9711. FS, CL, E,
    HP, TC, PG, BS, PA.

Rodeway Inn, 14th St.—79 rooms. 144 Fourteenth St.,

NW, Atlanta (30318). Tel. 873-4171. FS, CL, E, FU, P, BS, PA.

Rodeway Inn, Lenox—180 rooms. 3387 Lenox Rd., NW, Atlanta (30326). Tel. 261-5500. FS, CL, E, FU, P, PA.

Royal Inn of Atlanta, Airport—200 rooms. 301 Central Ave., Atlanta (30354). Tel. 763-2511. FS, CL, FU, HP, HC, SB, KF.

Sheraton Atlanta Inn—505 rooms. 590 West Peachtree St., NW, Atlanta (30308). Tel. 881-6000. FS, CL, E, HP, HC, SB.

Sheraton Biltmore Hotel—650 rooms. 817 West Peachtree St., Atlanta (30383). Tel. 881-9500. FS, CL, E, FU, P.

Sheraton Emory Inn—113 rooms. 1641 Clifton Rd., NE, Atlanta (30329). Tel. 636-0341. FS, CL, P, BS, PA.

Sheraton Inn, Atlanta Airport—372 rooms. 1325 Virginia Ave., Atlanta (30344). Tel. 768-6660. FS, CL, E, P, BS, PA.

Sheraton/Winchester Inn—132 rooms. I-285 & Ga. 3, Smyrna (30080). Tel. 432-8541. FS, CL, E, P, SB, PA.

Sky Host Inn—100 rooms. 1360 E. Virginia Ave., Atlanta (30344). Tel. 761-5201. FS, P, PA.

Sonesta Hotel, Tower Place—230 rooms. 3340 Peachtree Rd., near Lenox Square, Atlanta (30326). Tel. 262-7466. FS, CL, P, HC.

Squire Inn Downtown—102 rooms. 330 West Peachtree St., NW, Atlanta (30308). Tel. 525-2771. FS, CL, E, PA.

Squire Inn Northeast—194 rooms. 2115 Piedmont Rd., NE, Atlanta (30324). Tel. 876-4365. FS, CL, E, P, PA.

Squire Inn Northwest—199 rooms. 2767 Windy Hill Rd., SE, Marietta (30067). Tel. 432-3251. FS, CL, E, P, PA.

Squire Inn Sandy Springs—100 rooms. 5750 Roswell Rd.,

NW, Atlanta (30342). Tel. 252-5782. FS, CL, E, P, BS, PA.

Squire Inn South—124 rooms. 4730 South Expressway, Forest Park (30050). Tel. 361-6100. FS, FU, P, BS, PA.

Stone Mountain Inn—90 rooms. Hwy. 78, Stone Mountain Park, Stone Mountain (30086). Tel. 469-3311. FS, HP, GC, BS.

Stouffer's Pineisle—256 rooms. Lake Lanier Islands, P. O. Drawer 545, Buford (30518). Tel. 945-8955. FS, CL, E, HP, SB, GC, TC, GR, also riding, fishing, boating.

Tech Motel—125 rooms. 120 North Ave., NW, Atlanta (30313). Tel. 881-6788. FS, CL, FU, P, BS, PA.

Terrace Garden Inn—364 rooms. 3405 Lenox Rd., NE, Atlanta (30326). Tel. 261-9250; toll-free 800-323-9111. FS, CL, E, P, BS, TC.

Travelodge at Executive Park—208 rooms. 2061 N. Druid Hills Rd., Atlanta (30329). FS, CL, E, FU, HP, PA.

Unicoi Lodge and Conference Center—60 rooms, 20 cottages. P. O. Box 256, Helen (30545). Tel. 878-2201. FS, K, FU, PG, BS, lake and boating, swimming, fishing, hiking trails.

White House Inn—220 rooms. 70 Houston St., NE, Atlanta (30303). Tel. 659-2660. FS, CL, E, HP, BS, PA.

ADMISSIONS AND HOURS

ATTRACTION	PHONE NO.	HOURS	ADMISSION CHARGE
Atlanta Farmers' Market	366-6910	Every day from 7 A.M.	No.
Atlanta Historical Society -McElreath Hall	261-1837	Tues.–Sat. 10:30 A.M. to 4:30 P.M. Sun. 2 P.M. to 4:30 P.M. Closed Mon.	No.
-Swan House	233-2991	Hours same as above.	Yes.
-Tullie Smith House	262-1067	Hours same as above.	Yes.
Atlanta Memorial Arts Center -Museum of Art	892-3600	Mon.–Sat. 10 A.M. to 5 P.M. Sun. noon to 5 P.M. Center opened for evening performances.	No. Charge for special exhibits.
-Youth Museum	892-3600	June through Labor Day noon to 5 P.M. Other months 3 P.M. to 5 P.M.	No.

ADMISSIONS AND HOURS (cont'd)

ATTRACTION	PHONE NO.	HOURS	ADMISSION CHARGE
Atlanta Public Library	688-4636	Mon.–Fri. 9 A.M. to 9 P.M. Sat. 9 A.M. to 6 P.M. Sun. 2 to 6 P.M.	No.
Atlanta Zoo	658-7059	Mon.–Sat. 10 A.M. to 5 P.M. Sun. 11 A.M. to 7 P.M.	Yes–adults. No–16 and under.
Big Shanty Museum	427-2117	Every day 9:30 A.M. to 6 P.M.	Yes. Under 10, free.
Callaway Gardens	1-663-2281	Every day 7:30 A.M. to dusk.	Yes.
Coca-Cola Archives	897-2581	Mon.–Fri. 9 A.M. to 4:30 P.M.	No.
Cyclorama	627-4012	Every day 9:30 A.M. to 4:30 P.M. Shows every hour on the half hour.	Yes.

Dahlonega Gold Hills	266-1781	June through Oct, every day 10 A.M. to 6 P.M. April & May weekends, 10 A.M. to 6 P.M.	Yes.
Dahlonega Gold Museum	1-864-2257	Tues.–Sat. 9 A.M. to 5 P.M. Closed Mon. Sun. 2 P.M. to 5:30 P.M.	No.
Dr. Martin Luther King, Jr., Birthplace	524-4402	Tues.–Sat. 10:30 A.M. to 4 P.M. Sun. 1:30 P.M. to 4:30 P.M.	Yes.
-Ebenezer Baptist Church		Same as above.	Yes.
Emory University Museum	329-7322	Mon.–Fri. 10 A.M. to noon, 2 P.M. to 4 P.M. Sat. 2 P.M. to 4 P.M. Closed Sun.	No.
Emory University John Wesley Room	329-7322	Call in advance for hours.	No.

ADMISSIONS AND HOURS (cont'd)

ATTRACTION	PHONE NO.	HOURS	ADMISSION CHARGE
Etowah Indian Mounds	1-382-2704	Tues.–Sat. 9 A.M. to 5 P.M. Sun. 2 P.M. to 5:30 P.M. Closed Mon.	No.
Fernbank Science Center	378-4311	Open every day. Hours vary. Call in advance.	
-Planetarium			Yes.
-Forest			No.
-Museum			No.
-Observatory			No.
Fort Walker, Grant Park		Open every day.	No.
Fox Theatre	892-5685	Call in advance.	Contributions.
Georgia Archives Bldg.	656-2399	Mon.–Fri. 8 A.M. to 4:30 P.M. Sat. 9:30 A.M. to 3:30 P.M.	No.

Attraction	Phone	Hours	Admission
Georgia Governor's Mansion	261-1776	Call in advance.	No.
Georgia State Capitol Museum	656-2844	Mon.–Fri. 8 A.M. to 5 P.M. Closed weekends & holidays.	No.
Kennesaw Mountain Memorial	427-4686	9 A.M. to 5 P.M. every day.	No.
Kingdoms 3	474-1461	10 A.M. till dusk, every day.	Yes.
Lake Lanier Islands	945-6701	Open every day. Call in advance for individual attraction hours.	Yes.
Madison-Morgan Cultural Center	1-342-0520	9 A.M. to 5 P.M. weekdays.	Nominal.
-Casulon Plantation, Madison		Call Madison Cultural Center for tour information.	
Mathis Dairy	289-1433	Mon.–Sat. Call in advance.	No.

ADMISSIONS AND HOURS (cont'd)

ATTRACTION	PHONE NO.	HOURS	ADMISSION CHARGE
Monastery of the Holy Ghost, Conyers	483-8705	Call in advance for hours, information.	No.
Six Flags over Georgia	948-9290	Every day June, July, Aug. Weekends Apr., May, Sept., Oct.	Yes.
Stone Mountain Park, all attractions	469-9831	June through Sept. 10 A.M. to 9 P.M. Oct. through May 10 A.M. to 5:30 P.M.	Yes.
Underground Atlanta	522-5285	11 A.M. to 2 A.M.	Nominal.
Vinings Ridge Ski Area	432-9563	Mon.–Sat. 3 P.M. to 10:30 P.M. Sun. 1 P.M. to 5 P.M.	Yes.

Warm Springs	1-655-3511	Every day 9 A.M. to 5 P.M.	Yes.
Wren's Nest	753-8535	Mon.-Sat. 9:30 A.M. to 4 P.M. Sun. 2 P.M. to 5 P.M.	Yes.

Index